A BASIC SYSTEMS PROGRAM

# REFLEXES AND CONDITIONED REFLEXES

George L. Geis
*Center for Research on Learning and Teaching*
*University of Michigan*

William C. Stebbins
*Kresge Hearing Research Institute*
*University of Michigan*

Robert W. Lundin
*Chairman, Department of Psychology*
*University of the South*

The Study of Behavior
Volume 1—Part 1

Appleton-Century-Crofts
*Division of Meredith Publishing Company*
New York

Copyright © 1965 by

BASIC SYSTEMS, INC.

All rights reserved. Neither this program nor any part thereof may be reproduced in any form whatsoever without permission of the copyright owner.

PRINTED IN THE UNITED STATES OF AMERICA

### Dedication

*To our students
who are patiently teaching us
to write better programs*

# Preface

This programmed text was originally developed under a grant to Hamilton College by the Fund for the Advancement of Education of the Ford Foundation. This grant supported the development and testing of an entire program, designed for use in a first-year course in systematic psychology at the college level. The present volume was adapted from the first portion of that course, and represents the first publication for wider use of what is planned as a complete course.

Each unit of the program was used and validated in the introductory course at Hamilton College. Portions of the program, including that portion here published, have undergone repeated testing and revision under such conditions of use. The material in the present volume was further tested by Basic Systems, Inc., with selected groups of students drawn from classes at Barnard, Columbia, Fairleigh Dickinson, and Hunter Colleges. The final revision has been validated with freshman and sophomore students at Columbia's School of General Studies, and with introductory psychology students, as well as non-psychology postgraduates, at the University of Michigan. To the many students who provided data used in revising the program, and the instructors who helped us recruit and select these students, our thanks are due.

A description of the validation procedure, and the results obtained in testing, are available to teachers and researchers from the Programming Department, Appleton-Century-Crofts —— 440 Park Avenue South, New York, N.Y. 10016.

In the space provided we cannot adequately thank the many people who have contributed to this volume and to the series. A few names may serve as a sample, however. We express our deep appreciation to:

Mrs. Lawrence Yourtee, who typed and retyped literally thousands of pages of manuscript revisions.

Mr. Charles Peyser, who for several years was research assistant on the project.

Dr. Donald A. Cook and Mr. Stephen F. Knapp of Basic Systems, Inc., who aided in the substantial editing and revision of this volume.

The Fund for the Advancement of Education of the Ford Foundation, whose original sponsorship made the project possible.

Professor Fred S. Keller, whose teaching serves as a continual reminder of what a program should try to achieve.

## To the Teacher

This programmed textbook is designed to impart, in brief but intensive compass, a grasp of the basic principles of the reflex, and of reflex conditioning, as studied and brought into the realm of scientific psychology by Ivan Pavlov.

The treatment emphasizes an accurate description of the behavioral relations involved in studying reflexes and the formation of new reflexes through the pairing of stimuli. In achieving this aim, the student is exposed to the practical use of certain basic concepts of wide application in the scientific study of behavior; examples are the notions of threshold and latency, and their treatment as dependent variables, in the context of a functional approach which emphasizes the relation between independent and dependent variables.

The program can appropriately be assigned over a week, or at most two, in the early stages of a general or advanced general course, as well as in more specialized courses in learning, comparative psychology, or educational psychology. The emphasis of the program is on the acquisition of behavior. Students who complete the program should be well prepared for extensions into further topics such as extinction, generalization, discrimination and operant or instrumental learning.

It is our contention as authors of the program that the distinction between classical or Pavlovian (reflex) conditioning and operant (or instrumental) conditioning is a valid one and a very important first principle for an introductory course in psychology. Further, we feel that there is good evidence that this distinction between the types of conditioning is directly related to the physiologic difference between the autonomic and somatic systems. Consequently, in the treatment of reflex conditioning practically all of the examples of reflexes are autonomic and involve innervation of smooth muscle, gland, or cardiac muscle. We feel that reported instances of classical defense conditioning (e.g., foot withdrawal, finger withdrawal, eye blink, etc.) may be examples of operant conditioning (i.e., avoidance). However, the use of the program does not in any way preclude the instructor from presenting additional material on reflexes of his own choosing.

An examination will be found at the end of the volume, designed to cover the major concepts and principles taught by the program. The instructor facing a class whose students possess varying degrees of preparation may wish to employ this test as a screening device for selective assignment of the program. More often, he may wish to use the test as a pretest before assigning the program, and as a posttest afterwards, for the purposes of evaluating gains and motivating the student. Test results, based on either a single administration or use before and after the program, may also be used as the basis for review, discussion, and clarification.

# To the Student

## *About Psychology*

Psychology is the study of behavior. It deals with the effects of the environment upon an organism, be he man or mouse. The purpose of this program is to start you on a scientific account of the relationships between the behavior of organisms and the surrounding environment. When you have completed this program you should be able to apply some of the principles to familiar examples from your experience. You will probably have many questions about areas with which the program does not deal, and working with the program itself will raise other questions. If this program helps you to phrase those questions more carefully and exactly, one of its main purposes will have been well served.

## *About the Use of This Program*

This program is designed to guide you through the subject in a careful sequence of steps which makes for efficient learning. Each step is called a "frame," and each frame brings in something new. It also asks you to use this new material—which is carefully based on what you have already learned—in an *active response*. This means that you will be asked to complete a sentence, fill in a blank, check a multiple-choice question, label a drawing, or make some other brief response. It is best to make your response in the space provided in the frame itself. Do not use the length of the blank as a cue to the length of your answer. Sometimes you will need to write a phrase in a single blank. After you have made your response, you can check your answer with the correct answer which is next to each frame. Thus you will master the material in a step-by-step fashion, responding to each step, and checking each answer you write.

The frames of the program—which contain the material to study and the questions to answer—are on the left-hand side of each page, and are numbered in serial order. The answer to each frame is just to its right, and is printed in a shaded column to help you avoid glancing at the answer before you write your own. Does it matter if you peek at the answer before you try your own? Yes, it does—you will not learn as well. This program has been tried out on many students, and revised on the basis of their results. We know, therefore, that you will get most frames right on your own, and that if you write your answer to each one, you will learn well. Many students find it helpful to cover the answer with an index card, which you can slide down the answer column as you progress through the frames.

Despite our efforts, and yours, you will probably make an occasional error. When this happens, check the answer given and satisfy yourself that you understand it. If you think it better than yours, correct your own response before proceeding.

The program is organized into relatively brief chapters. Each one may take you anywhere from half an hour to an hour to complete, and it is best to work on the program when you can complete an entire chapter at one sitting.

*Remember:* You will learn in steps, respond to each step, and check your answer right away—*after* your response! This is not a test and there are no trick questions. After mastering this program in the proper manner, you will understand some important principles of psychology.

At the back of this program, you will notice several panels. You will be asked to respond to the material contained in them. These panels contain critical information which, because of length and/or complexity, cannot be included in the body of the program. Note also that these panels are perforated to facilitate their removal and use.

As you take the program, you will be required to refer to these panels. The directions at these points will be in a form such as "REFER TO PANEL A." When required to refer to a panel, tear it out and use it until directed otherwise.

# Contents

R-1  Reflexes                                                          3

R-2  Effective Stimuli                                                15

R-3  Measuring Reflex Strength: Latency and Magnitude                 24

R-4  Stimulus—Response Relationships                                  34

R-5  The Principle of Reflex Conditioning (Pavlovian Conditioning)    42

R-6  Forming Conditioned Reflexes                                     51

R-7  Number of Pairings as an Independent Variable                    56

R-8  Temporal Patterns in Conditioning                                73

R-9  Higher Order Conditioning                                        95

    Panels                                                          109

    Terminal Examination                                            115

# REFLEXES AND CONDITIONED REFLEXES

# R-1

## Reflexes

1

Things happen in our *environment*. For example:
- a. Juicy steak is placed on the tongue.
- b. A light is shined in the eye.

These things that happen affect our *behavior* in certain ways. For example:
- c. Saliva flows in the mouth.
- d. Pupil of the eye becomes smaller.

The placing of steak in the mouth probably is followed by:
- ☐ saliva flow
- ☐ decrease in size of the pupil

Shining a light in the eye is followed by:
- ☐ saliva flow
- ☐ decrease in size of the pupil

| | saliva flow |
| | decrease in size of the pupil |

------------------------------

2

An event in the environment is called a *stimulus* (plural *stimuli*). Parts of our behavior are called *responses*.

The increase of temperature in a room is a:
- ☐ stimulus
- ☐ response

This leads to perspiring, which is a:
- ☐ stimulus
- ☐ response

| stimulus |
| response |

------------------------------

4 / Reflexes and Conditioned Reflexes

3

Which is the stimulus?
- ☐ cold wind
- ☐ weeping

Which is the response?
- ☐ "goose pimples" appear
- ☐ onion placed under nose

| cold wind |
| "goose pimples" appear |

---

4

Psychologists are interested when stimuli and responses are *related* in some way.

CHECK the sentence that seems to express a relationship between stimulus and response:
- ☐ As he walked down the hill, a cool wind began to blow.
- ☐ As the cool wind blew, "goose pimples" appeared on his arms.

As the cool wind blew, goose pimples appeared on his arms.

---

5

This relationship between a stimulus and a response is called a *reflex*. Here is an example:

If a light shines in your eye, the pupil contracts (becomes smaller).

In this reflex, the stimulus is the _____ and the response is the _____ of the _____.

light
contraction (of the) pupil

---

6

In describing this reflex, we say that:

*Light elicits pupil contraction.*

The subject of this sentence is the name of a:
- ☐ stimulus
- ☐ response

stimulus

---

**7**

To *elicit* means "to draw out, to draw forth, to bring forth." The word *elicit* is a(n):
- ☐ noun
- ☐ verb
- ☐ adjective

> verb

---

**8**

Here is another example of a reflex:
*An onion placed under the nose causes tears to flow.*
The response in this reflex is _____.

> weeping *or* flow of tears

---

**9**

*An onion placed under the nose causes tears to flow from the eyes.*
In this reflex, the onion is a(n) _____.
The weeping is a(n) _____.

> stimulus
> response

---

**10**

*A rotten odor elicits vomiting.*
What word in the sentence tells that the stimulus and response are related in a reflex? _____

> elicits

---

**11**

If you receive an electric shock, your heart rate may increase.
WRITE a sentence using the following terms:
  elicits
  electric shock
  heart rate increase

...........................

> Electric shock elicits heart rate increase.

6 / Reflexes and Conditioned Reflexes

**12**

*Light "brings forth" pupil contraction.*
REPLACE the phrase *brings forth* with the correct technical term. _____

| elicits |

---

**13**

The general description of a reflex is:
   A(n) _____ elicits a(n) _____.

| stimulus   response |

---

**14**

CHECK the appropriate response for each of the following stimuli:

*Stimuli*              *Responses*
Steak on the tongue    ☐ tears
   elicits:            ☐ pupil contraction
                       ☐ salivation

An onion under the nose   ☐ tears
   elicits:               ☐ pupil contraction
                          ☐ salivation

| salivation
tears |

---

**15**

Steak in the mouth does *not* elicit: (CHECK ONE)
   ☐ salivation
   ☐ weeping

| weeping |

---

**16**

What technical term do we use to describe the relationship between stimulus and response in a reflex? (Hint: The term is a verb meaning "to draw out, to draw forth, to bring forth.")
_____

| to elicit *or* elicit *or* elicits |

17

CHECK the stimulus that would elicit each of the following two responses:
    Heart rate increase:
        ☐ light
        ☐ an onion
        ☐ shock
    Pupil contraction:
        ☐ light
        ☐ an onion
        ☐ shock

shock

light

---

18

Light does *not* elicit:
    ☐ heart rate increase
    ☐ pupil contraction

heart rate increase

---

19

To predict what response will be elicited in a reflex, it helps if you know what _____ was presented.

stimulus

---

20

In a reflex, a specific stimulus elicits its own particular _____.

response

---

21

In a reflex, a stimulus _____ a response.

elicits

---

## 8 / Reflexes and Conditioned Reflexes

**22**

Does a light normally elicit weeping?
- ☐ yes
- ☐ no

no

Does the relationship between light and weeping normally make up a reflex?
- ☐ yes
- ☐ no

no

---

**23**

Do any stimulus and any response form a reflex?
- ☐ yes
- ☐ no

no

---

**24**

Only when a stimulus elicits a response can we speak of a(n) _____.

reflex

---

**25**

A freezing temperature _____ shivering. This relationship between stimulus and response is called a(n) _____.

elicits

reflex

---

**26**

When a specific _____ elicits a(n) _____, the relationship is called a(n) _____.

stimulus
response
reflex

---

**27**

When a stimulus elicits a response, which comes first in time?
- ☐ the stimulus
- ☐ the response

the stimulus

---

28

When we speak of a *reflex*, the two things we observe are the _____ and the _____.

stimulus   response

- - - - - - - - - - - - - - - - - - - - - - - -

29

To discover whether a particular stimulus is an eliciting stimulus for a given reflex, we present the stimulus and observe whether the _____ occurs.

response

- - - - - - - - - - - - - - - - - - - - - - - -

30

If the stimulus elicits the response, the relationship of stimulus and response is called a(n) _____.

reflex

- - - - - - - - - - - - - - - - - - - - - - - -

31

In a reflex, which comes first?
- ☐ stimulus
- ☐ response

stimulus

- - - - - - - - - - - - - - - - - - - - - - - -

32

We have used the word *stimuli* to describe parts of, or changes in parts of:
- ☐ behavior
- ☐ the environment

the environment

- - - - - - - - - - - - - - - - - - - - - - - -

33

Our technical term for parts of the environment, or changes in parts of the environment, is _____.

stimulus *or* stimuli

- - - - - - - - - - - - - - - - - - - - - - - -

10 / Reflexes and Conditioned Reflexes

34

A steady light can be called a stimulus because it is a:
- ☐ part of the environment
- ☐ change in part of the environment

A soft sound becoming loud can also be called a stimulus because it is a:
- ☐ part of the environment
- ☐ change in part of the environment

part of the environment

change in part of the environment

---

35

A stimulus is a part of, or a change in a part of, the _____.

environment

---

36

A part of, or a change in a part of, the *environment* is called a(n) _____.

In like manner, a part of, or a change in a part of, *behavior* must be the definition of a(n) _____.

stimulus

response

---

37

*Stimulus* is a technical term used in describing the environment.

*Response* is a technical term used in describing _____.

behavior

---

38

A stimulus is a part of, or a _____ in a part of, the environment.

change

---

39

A response is a _____ of, or a change in a _____ of, the behavior. (The same word goes in both blanks.)

part
part

---

**40**

When a given stimulus elicits a specific response, the relationship is called a(n) _____.

| reflex

---

**41**

DEFINE a *stimulus*.

_____

| A stimulus is a part of, or a change in a part of, the environment.
| (or equivalent answer)

---

**42**

DEFINE a *response*.

_____

| A response is a part of, or a change in a part of behavior.
| (or equivalent answer)

---

**43**

In a reflex, the first event is the presentation of the _____.

| stimulus

The second event is the elicitation of the _____.

| response

---

**44**

In a reflex, we say that the stimulus _____ the response.

| elicits

---

**45**

REVIEW AND PREVIEW

You have learned some important terms and concepts. For example, you know that the psychologist analyzes the environment into more specific parts called _____.

| stimuli

You also know that the psychologist analyzes behavior into more specific parts called _____.

| responses

12 / Reflexes and Conditioned Reflexes

46

You have become familiar with one specific relationship between stimuli and responses. That relationship exists when a stimulus elicits a response, and we call it a _____.

> reflex

---

47

In all the reflexes we have considered, the first event in time was the:
- ☐ stimulus
- ☐ response

> stimulus

and the second event to occur was the:
- ☐ stimulus
- ☐ response

> response

---

48

We have used a special term to describe the relationship between the stimulus and the response in a reflex. We say:

"In a reflex, the stimulus _____ the response."

> elicits

---

49

But we have *not* discussed "where reflexes come from." Some, for example, may be present at birth. Which reflex might you expect to find in a newborn baby?
- ☐ having "goose pimples" when hearing the national anthem
- ☐ sucking when lips and tongue are stimulated

> sucking when lips and tongue are stimulated

---

**50**

The reaction of having "goose pimples" when hearing the national anthem is *not* present at birth. Yet it is a reflex. The stimulus is _____ and the response is _____.

| hearing national anthem
| having "goose pimples"

---

**51**

Given the stimulus (national anthem) and the response ("goose pimples"), there remains to be explained how the stimulus comes to _____ the response.

elicit

---

**52**

When we have explained such cases, we will have some understanding of both unlearned and learned _____ (plural).

reflexes

---

**53**

We know that neither kind of reflex—unlearned or learned—will occur unless we first present a(n) _____.

stimulus

---

**54**

When the dinner bell rings, you may start salivating. When you taste a juicy steak, you may salivate. Which case sounds like an unlearned reflex?

☐ dinner bell rings and you salivate
☐ you taste steak and you salivate

you taste steak and you salivate

---

**55**

In the foregoing example, which reflex was unlearned?

☐ salivation to steak
☐ salivation to dinner bell

salivation to steak

---

## 14 / Reflexes and Conditioned Reflexes

56

*Dinner bell elicits salivation.*
This reflex is:
☐ unlearned
☐ learned

learned

---

57

Generally speaking, the psychologist studies the relationship between the environment and the behavior of an organism.

The important parts of the environment, he calls _____ (plural).

stimuli

The important parts of behavior he calls _____ (plural).

responses

---

58

Some reflex relationships between stimuli and responses are unlearned, while others are learned.

COMPLETE the entry of checks in the table below to indicate which reflexes are unlearned and which are learned:

| STIMULUS | RESPONSE | TYPE OF REFLEX Unlearned | Learned | | Unlearned | Learned |
|---|---|---|---|---|---|---|
| cinder in eye | blinking | X | | | (X) | |
| dinner bell | salivation | | X | | | (X) |
| embarrassing situation | blushing | | | | | X |
| onion under the nose | weeping | | | | X | |
| food in mouth | salivation | | | | X | |
| national anthem | goose pimples | | | | | X |
| light in eye | pupil contraction | | | | X | |
| electric shock | increase in heart rate | | | | X | |
| sound of dentist's drill | sweating and trembling | | | | | X |

# R-2

## Effective Stimuli

1

Suppose someone far across the room from you held an onion in his hand. Do you think your eyes would water?
- ☐ probably
- ☐ probably not

    probably not

------------------------------

2

As he walked toward you, the odor of the onion would become stronger. If he held the onion under your nose, you might start to weep because the odor is then:
- ☐ strong
- ☐ weak

    strong

------------------------------

3

If a stimulus is weak enough, it will fail to _____ any response.

    elicit

------------------------------

4

Which stimulus will not elicit a response?
- ☐ a strong stimulus
- ☐ a weak stimulus

    a weak stimulus

------------------------------

5

If we decrease or turn down a very intense stimulus to a low enough value, it will no longer elicit any _____.

    response

------------------------------

## 16 / Reflexes and Conditioned Reflexes

**6**

The strong odor of onion elicits weeping. A weak odor of onion *does not* elicit weeping.

What determines whether weeping occurs?
_____

    the strength *or* intensity of the odor (stimulus)

---

**7**

To state this question another way, we might ask: In studying the pupillary reflex, how _____ a light is required to elicit pupil contraction?

    intense *or* bright *or* strong

---

**8**

If we start with a weak light that elicits no response, and we make it gradually brighter and brighter, we will reach a point at which the light will _____ pupil contraction. We call that point the *threshold*.

    elicit

If the intensity of a light is below the threshold, the light (☐ will ☐ will not) elicit pupil contraction. If the intensity is above the threshold, the light (☐ will ☐ will not) elicit pupil contraction.

    will not

    will

---

**9**

What do we call the point at which a stimulus (light) will elicit a response (pupil contraction)?
_____

    the threshold

---

**10**

A stimulus below the threshold (☐ will ☐ will not) elicit a response.

    will not

---

**11**

In any given reflex, the threshold refers to the intensity of a(n) _____ just sufficient to elicit a(n) _____.

    stimulus
    response

## Effective Stimuli / 17

**12**

If we gradually increase the intensity of a stimulus, we reach a point at which the stimulus will elicit a response. That point is known as the _____.

threshold

---

**13**

Every reflex has a threshold. If you know the threshold value, you know how intense to make the _____ in order to _____.
(phrase)

stimulus   elicit the response

---

**14**

Suppose a light of 6 units of intensity is the least intense light that will elicit pupil contraction. The threshold for this reflex is ___ units.

6

---

**15**

The minimal value of a stimulus sufficient to elicit a response is called the _____.

threshold

---

**16**

In the previous example: If the threshold is 6 units, then a stimulus of 4 units would be (☐ above the threshold   ☐ below the threshold). Would the stimulus of 4 units elicit a response?
  ☐ yes
  ☐ no

below the threshold

no

---

**17**

And if the light were of 8 units intensity, then it would be (☐ above   ☐ below) the threshold for pupillary contraction. A light of 8 units (☐ would   ☐ would not) elicit contraction.

above
would

---

18 / Reflexes and Conditioned Reflexes

18

In a reflex, the threshold is the lowest intensity value of a stimulus sufficient to elicit a particular _____.

response

---

19

DEFINE the term *threshold*. _____

Threshold is the minimal value of a stimulus sufficient to elicit a response.
(or equivalent answer)

---

20

The word *limen* is synonymous with the word *threshold*. A stimulus of a value below the limen will not _____.

elicit a response

---

21

If stimulus intensity is above the threshold for a given reflex, then we could also say it is:
  ☐ above the limen
  ☐ below the limen

above the limen

---

22

A synonym for the word *threshold* is the word _____.

limen

---

23

If *sub* means *below* and *limen* means *threshold*, then *subliminal* refers to a stimulus that is below the _____.

threshold *or* limen

---

24

If the limen or threshold is 6 units, then a value of ____ units would be subliminal.

any number below 6

---

Effective Stimuli / 19

25

If the limen is 6 units, then a stimulus with a value of 2 units is a(n) _____ stimulus.

subliminal

---

26

If *subliminal* means *below threshold*, and *supra* means *above*, what does *supraliminal* mean? _____

above threshold *or* limen

---

27

If 6 units is liminal, 7 units should be _____ liminal.

supraliminal

---

28

Which stimulus will *not* elicit a response?
☐ subliminal
☐ supraliminal

subliminal

---

29

Will a supraliminal stimulus elicit a response?
☐ yes
☐ no

yes

---

**READ THROUGH PANEL R-2-1 BEFORE GOING ON TO THE FOLLOWING ITEMS.**

---

30

(Refer to Panel R-2-1.)

The panel reports a study on the pupillary reflex. What stimulus was used? _____

light *or* a spot of light flashed in the eye

---

20 / Reflexes and Conditioned Reflexes

31

(Refer to Panel R-2-1.)

The experimenter varied the (☐ duration   ☐ intensity) of the light.

intensity

---

32

(Refer to Panel R-2-1.)

In the dark, the diameter of the pupil is 6.5 millimeters. At 0.000001 foot-lambert of intensity or less, the diameter of the pupil is:
  ☐ about the same
  ☐ very much smaller

about the same

---

33

An intensity of less than 0.000001 foot-lambert of light is (☐ above   ☐ below) the threshold for the pupillary reflex.

below

---

34

For the pupillary reflex, a light intensity of less than 0.000001 foot-lambert is:
  ☐ supraliminal
  ☐ subliminal

subliminal

---

35

(Refer to Panel R-2-1.)

As the light gets brighter, what happens to the size (diameter) of the pupil? _____

The diameter of the pupil decreases.

---

36

(Refer to Panel R-2-1.)

At 10 foot-lamberts of intensity, the diameter of the pupil is about _____ millimeters.

3

---

37

The greater the intensity of the light, the more the pupil contracts. In the brightest light, the pupil is (☐ least  ☐ most) contracted, and the diameter of the pupil is (☐ largest  ☐ smallest).

most
smallest

---

38

Which produces a greater change in pupil size?
- ☐ increasing the light intensity from a subliminal value to 8 units
- ☐ increasing the light intensity from a subliminal value to 10 units

increasing the light intensity from a subliminal value to 10 units

---

39

In the pupillary reflex:
The stimulus is the intensity of the _____.
The contraction in pupil size is the _____.

light
response

---

40

The response (contraction) to light is greatest when the intensity of the stimulus is (☐ highest  ☐ lowest).

highest

---

41

In other words, increasing the intensity of the light has what effect on the response? _____

increases the response

---

42

When two stimuli are both above threshold for a given reflex, the stronger stimulus will elicit a(n) _____ response.

stronger
(or equivalent answer)

---

## 22 / Reflexes and Conditioned Reflexes

**43**

Usually, *intensity* refers to the strength of the stimulus and *magnitude* refers to the strength of the response. Therefore, we would say that as the intensity of a stimulus is increased, the magnitude of the _____ increases.

response

---

**44**

In general, the magnitude of the response is dependent on the intensity of the _____.

stimulus

---

**45**

One measure of a response is its magnitude. The magnitude of the response is directly related to the _____ of the _____.

intensity (of the) stimulus

---

**46**

The _____ of a response is related to the intensity of the stimulus that elicits it.

magnitude

---

**47**

We measure the salivary response in terms of the quantity of saliva elicited. This is a measure of the _____ of the response.

magnitude

---

**48**

In the pupillary reflex, the magnitude of the response (the extent of the pupil contraction) will depend on the _____ of the light stimulus.

intensity

---

**49**

Increasing the light intensity will have what effect on the response? _____

It will increase the magnitude of the response.

---

50

If there is a decrease in the _____ of the light stimulus, there will be a(n) _____ in the magnitude of the pupil contraction (response).

intensity
decrease

---

51

The _____ of the elicited response is dependent upon the _____ of the _____.

magnitude
intensity (of the) stimulus

---

52

If an experimenter increases the intensity of the stimulus, the magnitude of the elicited response:
- ☐ increases
- ☐ decreases

increases

If the experimenter decreases stimulus intensity, the response magnitude:
- ☐ increases
- ☐ decreases

decreases

---

53

Every reflex has a threshold. A stimulus whose intensity is below the threshold:
- ☐ will elicit the response
- ☐ will not elicit the response

will not elicit the response

A supraliminal stimulus:
- ☐ will elicit the response
- ☐ will not elicit the response

will elicit the response

---

54

A stimulus above threshold for a given reflex can also be called _____.

supraliminal

Increasing the intensity of such a stimulus will generally increase the _____ of the response.

magnitude

---

# R-3

## Measuring Reflex Strength: Latency and Magnitude

**1**

It is possible to change the (☐ intensity  ☐ magnitude) of a supraliminal stimulus. Such a change changes the (☐ intensity  ☐ magnitude) of the response.

intensity

magnitude

---

**2**

The magnitude of the response varies with the _____ of the _____.

intensity (of the) stimulus

---

**3**

Which response has the longer time between the presentation of the stimulus and the occurrence of the response?
- ☐ *a*. Salivation begins 4 seconds after the food touches the tongue.
- ☐ *b*. Pupil contraction begins 1/10 second after light shines in the eye.

The time between the presentation of the stimulus and the occurrence of the response is called the *latency* of the response.

What is the latency in each of the two examples above?
- *a*. _____ second(s).
- *b*. _____ second(s).

*a*.

4 (seconds)
1/10 (second)

---

**4**

The greater the amount of time elapsing between stimulus and response, the (☐ longer  ☐ shorter) is the latency.

longer

---

24

## 5

The latency of a response is the elapsed _____ between the stimulus and the response.

time

---

## 6

The latency of a response is the time between the presentation of the _____ and the occurrence of a _____.

stimulus
response

---

## 7

The elapsed time between the onset of a stimulus and the initiation of a response is called the _____.

latency

---

## 8

Picture the second hand on a watch or clock. A light is turned on when the hand is at 30 seconds; the subject's pupil begins to contract at 31 seconds. The latency of pupillary contraction would be _____ (two words).

one second

---

## 9

Suppose that we record the time when lemon juice is put on a subject's tongue. Then we record the time when the first drop of saliva occurs. The difference between these two times is the _____ of the salivary response.

latency

---

## 10

DEFINE the term *latency*. _____

Latency is the time between (the presentation of) a stimulus and (the occurrence of) a response. (or equivalent answer)

26 / Reflexes and Conditioned Reflexes

**11**

Two things are *directly related* when an increase in one brings about an increase in the other.

Increasing heat causes the mercury in a thermometer to rise. Therefore, heat and the movement of mercury may be said to be _____.

directly related

---

**12**

In a reflex, as the intensity of the stimulus is increased, the magnitude of the response is (☐ increased ☐ decreased).

increased

---

**13**

Therefore, stimulus intensity and response magnitude are _____ related.

directly

---

**14**

If stimulus intensity is decreased, the magnitude of the response will _____.

decrease

---

**15**

There is a direct relationship between the _____ of a response and the _____ of the stimulus.

magnitude   intensity

---

**16**

When two things are directly related, an increase in one is accompanied by a(n) _____ in the other. Conversely, a decrease in one is accompanied by a(n) _____ in the other.

increase

decrease

---

**17**

The intensity of a stimulus and the magnitude of the response are _____ related.

directly

---

18

Let's take a different situation.

If you lost weight by exercising, then as you increased the amount of exercise you did, your weight would _____.

decrease

---

19

The opposite of a direct relationship is an *inverse relationship*. In an *inverse* relationship, an increase in one thing would be accompanied by a(n) (☐ increase  ☐ decrease) in the other.

decrease

---

20

In the previous example, your weight and the amount of exercise you did would be (☐ directly  ☐ inversely) related.

inversely

---

21

Latency is inversely related to the stimulus intensity. Therefore, as the intensity of a stimulus is increased, the latency of the response will:
    ☐ increase
    ☐ decrease

decrease

---

22

A weak stimulus elicits a response with a long _____. Therefore, response latency and stimulus intensity are _____ related.

latency
inversely (indirectly is
  wrong)

---

23

A strong stimulus elicits a response with a (☐ long  ☐ short) latency.

short

---

## 24

The intensity of the stimulus is inversely related to the _____ of the _____.

> latency (of the) response

---

## 25

(Refer to Panel R-3-1, Figure I.)

In Figure I, changing the stimulus intensity from 1 to 2 *units* changes the value of A (on the vertical axis) from 25 to _____ units.

> 75

---

## 26

(Refer to Panel R-3-1, Figure I.)

In other words, the relationship between intensity and A is (☐ direct  ☐ inverse).

> direct

---

## 27

(Refer to Panel R-3-1, Figure I.)

You can guess, therefore, that A stands for response _____.

LABEL the vertical axis correctly on the panel.

> magnitude
> A = Response Magnitude

---

## 28

What do we mean when we say that the relationship between stimulus intensity and response magnitude is a direct one? _____

> We mean that an increase in stimulus intensity produces an increase in response magnitude, and a decrease in stimulus intensity produces a decrease in response magnitude.
> (or equivalent answer)

29

(Refer to Panel R-3-1, Figure II.)

When stimulus intensity is 1, B is _____.          40
When stimulus intensity is 2, B is _____.          20
When stimulus intensity is 3, B is _____.          10
As stimulus intensity increases, what happens to
B? _____                                            B decreases.
This relationship is (☐ direct  ☐ inverse).       inverse
B stands for response _____.                       latency
LABEL the vertical axis correctly.                 B = Response Latency

------------------------------------------------

30

(Refer to Panel R-3-1, Figure II.)

A decrease in response latency from 40 to 20 units
is brought about by an increase in stimulus intensity from _____ to _____ units.                    1 (to) 2

------------------------------------------------

31

(Refer to Panel R-3-1, Figure II.)

Between stimulus intensity and response latency
there is a(n) _____ relationship.                  inverse

------------------------------------------------

32

(Refer to Panel R-3-1.)

We will now consider Figures I and II together.
In both figures, stimulus intensity is plotted on
the (☐ horizontal axis  ☐ vertical axis).         horizontal axis

------------------------------------------------

33

(Refer to Panel R-3-1.)

Latency and magnitude are both plotted on the
(☐ horizontal axis  ☐ vertical axis).             vertical axis
Both of these terms refer to measures of the
(☐ stimulus  ☐ response).                         response

------------------------------------------------

30 / Reflexes and Conditioned Reflexes

**34**

(Refer to Panel R-3-1.)

When studying behavior, we often measure several things at once. Figures I and II report results from the same experiment. We have measured the stimulus in _____ (how many) way(s), and we have measured the response in _____ (how many) way(s).

1
2

---

**35**

(Refer to Panel R-3-1.)

SUMMARIZE the results of the experiment by completing the following table:

| Stimulus Intensity | Response Magnitude | Response Latency |
|---|---|---|
| 0 | 0 | — |
| 1 | 25 | 40 |
| 2 |   |   |
| 3 |   |   |

| Response Magnitude | Response Latency |
|---|---|
| (0) | (—) |
| (25) | (40) |
| 75 | 20 |
| 100 | 10 |

---

**36**

As stimulus intensity increases, what happens to response magnitude? _____

Response magnitude increases.

As stimulus intensity increases, what happens to the latency of the response? _____

Response latency becomes shorter (decreases).

---

**37**

Response magnitude varies (☐ directly ☐ inversely) with stimulus intensity.

directly

---

**38**

Response latency varies (☐ directly ☐ inversely) with stimulus intensity.

inversely

---

Measuring Reflex Strength: Latency and Magnitude / 31

39

Suppose a stimulus elicits a response with a long latency. You might predict that the magnitude of that response will be relatively (☐ large ☐ small).

small

- - - - - - - - - - - - - - - - - - - - - - - -

40

(Refer to Panel R-3-1, Figure I.)

In Figure I, does a stimulus below 0.5 unit of intensity elicit a response?
 ☐ yes
 ☐ no

no

- - - - - - - - - - - - - - - - - - - - - - - -

41

(Refer to Panel R-3-1, Figure I.)

Responses are elicited by stimuli above _____ unit(s) of intensity.

0.5

- - - - - - - - - - - - - - - - - - - - - - - -

42

(Refer to Panel R-3-1, Figure I.)

What is the threshold value of the stimulus in the reflex we are studying?
 _____ units(s) of _____

0.5 (unit of) stimulus intensity

- - - - - - - - - - - - - - - - - - - - - - - -

43

(Refer to Panel R-3-1.)

CHECK the correct boxes:

| Stimulus Intensity | Subliminal | Supraliminal |
|---|---|---|
| 0.05 | ☐ | ☐ |
| 0.25 | ☐ | ☐ |
| 0.45 | ☐ | ☐ |
| 0.65 | ☐ | ☐ |
| 0.85 | ☐ | ☐ |

| Subliminal | Supraliminal |
|---|---|
| ☒ | ☐ |
| ☒ | ☐ |
| ☒ | ☐ |
| ☐ | ☒ |
| ☐ | ☒ |

- - - - - - - - - - - - - - - - - - - - - - - -

32 / Reflexes and Conditioned Reflexes

44

Stimulus intensity is plotted on the (☐ horizontal ☐ vertical) axis of a graph.

Response magnitude and response latency are plotted on the (☐ horizontal ☐ vertical) axis of a graph.

horizontal

vertical

------------------------------

45

In general, measures of the response are plotted on the _____ axis, while measures of the stimulus are plotted on the _____ axis.

vertical
horizontal

------------------------------

46

As stimulus intensity increases, response magnitude (☐ increases ☐ decreases).

As stimulus intensity decreases, the latency (☐ increases ☐ decreases).

increases

increases

------------------------------

47

The relationship between stimulus intensity and response magnitude is _____.

The relationship between stimulus intensity and response latency is _____.

direct

inverse

------------------------------

48

Assume that we present a stimulus and no response occurs.

What is the value of the response magnitude?
_____

This stimulus would be (☐ above  ☐ below) threshold.

It would therefore be termed:
 ☐ subliminal
 ☐ supraliminal

Could we measure a latency in this case?
 ☐ yes
 ☐ no

------------------------------

0

below

subliminal

no

# R-4

## Stimulus-Response Relationships

1

In an experiment, a psychologist increases the intensity of a light, then measures the change in pupillary response. Which event occurs first?
- ☐ light intensity is increased
- ☐ pupil contraction is measured

*Answer: light intensity is increased*

---

2

A psychologist measures the latency of a response at one stimulus intensity. Then he decreases the intensity of the stimulus and again measures response latency.

In the second case, the latency is likely to be:
- ☐ longer
- ☐ shorter

*Answer: longer*

Which does the psychologist change directly?
- ☐ stimulus intensity
- ☐ response latency

*Answer: stimulus intensity*

Which changes as a result?
- ☐ stimulus intensity
- ☐ response latency

*Answer: response latency*

---

3

A subject's heart rate may increase when the experimenter "turns up" the shock. Which sentence describes the situation best?
- ☐ The heart rate depends on the shock.
- ☐ The shock intensity depends on the heart rate.

*Answer: The heart rate depends on the shock.*

---

4

The name *independent variable* is given to the factor that the experimenter changes directly. The name *dependent variable* is given to the resulting changes that depend upon what was done.

If we study the way in which the concentration of lemon juice on the tongue affects the amount of saliva secreted by a dog, the independent variable is:
- ☐ amount of salivation
- ☐ concentration of lemon juice

The dependent variable is:
- ☐ amount of salivation
- ☐ concentration of lemon juice

concentration of lemon juice

amount of salivation

------

5

If we study the effect of the size of print used in a book upon the speed at which the book can be read, print size is the (☐ dependent ☐ independent) variable and reading speed is the (☐ dependent ☐ independent) variable.

independent

dependent

------

6

The response of a subject depends upon the stimulus. The experimenter can present and vary the stimulus as he pleases. The stimulus is the _____ variable, and the dependent variable is the _____.

independent

response

------

36 / Reflexes and Conditioned Reflexes

7

Response magnitude and response latency are measures of the behavior of the subject that we are investigating. They are both _____ variables.

    dependent

To change these behaviors, the experimenter must change stimulus intensity. Stimulus intensity is a(n):
    ☐ dependent variable
    ☐ independent variable

    independent variable

---

8

Here is the title of a psychological study: "The effect of Vitamin A dosage on accuracy of night vision."

The independent variable is:
    ☐ accuracy of night vision
    ☐ Vitamin A dosage

    Vitamin A dosage

The dependent variable is:
    ☐ accuracy of night vision
    ☐ Vitamin A dosage

    accuracy of night vision

---

9

The experimenter manipulates the (☐ dependent ☐ independent) variable and notes the resulting changes in the (☐ dependent ☐ independent) variable.

    independent
    dependent

---

10

The independent variable in psychology usually refers to (☐ a change in the environment ☐ the behavior of the subject).

    a change in the environment

The dependent variable refers to (☐ a change in the environment ☐ the behavior of the subject).

    the behavior of the subject

---

11

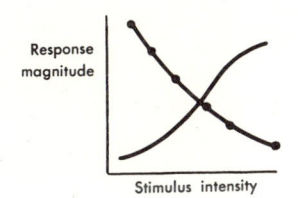

[Figure: Response magnitude vs Stimulus intensity]

In this figure, the dependent variable is plotted along the (☐ horizontal ☐ vertical) axis and the independent variable is plotted along the (☐ horizontal ☐ vertical) axis.

vertical

horizontal

- - - - - - - - - - - - - - - - - - - -

12

Here is another figure you have seen before:

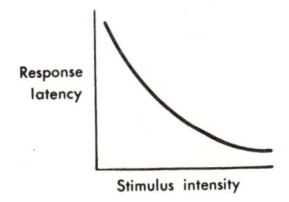

[Figure: Response latency vs Stimulus intensity]

In this figure, the dependent variable is plotted along the (☐ horizontal ☐ vertical) axis and the independent variable is plotted along the (☐ horizontal ☐ vertical) axis.

vertical

horizontal

- - - - - - - - - - - - - - - - - - - -

13

Often when we graph the results of a study, what variable do we plot on the vertical axis? _____

What variable do we plot on the horizontal axis? _____

dependent variable

independent variable

- - - - - - - - - - - - - - - - - - - -

38 / Reflexes and Conditioned Reflexes

14

An experiment is performed to study the time taken to eat a sandwich as a function of previous hours without food.

"Time to eat a sandwich" is the:
☐ dependent variable
☐ independent variable

"Previous hours without food" is the:
☐ dependent variable
☐ independent variable

Using the two phrases above, LABEL the axes of the figure below appropriately for presenting the results of the study:

| dependent variable

| independent variable

| Time to eat a sandwich (y-axis), Previous hours without food (x-axis)

---

15

In this figure:

(Response magnitude on y-axis, Stimulus intensity on x-axis)

The dependent variable is _____ _____ and the independent variable is _____ _____.

response magnitude
stimulus intensity

16

In this figure:

The dependent variable is \_\_\_\_\_ \_\_\_\_\_ and the independent variable is \_\_\_\_\_ \_\_\_\_\_.

| response latency
| stimulus intensity

---

17

Suppose that a study investigated *number of drops of saliva* as a function of *concentration of lemon juice* on the tongue. The independent variable would be \_\_\_\_\_.
The dependent variable would be \_\_\_\_\_.

| concentration of lemon juice
| number of drops of saliva

---

18

LABEL the two axes of the graph appropriately for this study of the *number of drops of saliva* as a function of the *concentration of lemon juice*:

| Number of drops of saliva
| Concentration of lemon juice

---

19

A graph is a quick and pictorial way of representing some types of data. We often also use symbols as shorthand. The symbol S stands for stimulus. Obviously, the symbol for response is \_\_\_\_\_.

| R

---

40 / Reflexes and Conditioned Reflexes

**20**

S = _____
R = _____

stimulus
response

- - - - - - - - - - - - - - - - - - - - - - - -

**21**

A reflex is defined as the elicitation of a(n) _____ by a(n) _____

response *or* R
stimulus *or* S

- - - - - - - - - - - - - - - - - - - - - - - -

**22**

In this notation:

$$S \longrightarrow R$$

the arrow from S to R is read *elicits*.
WRITE the expression above (S ⟶ R) as a complete English sentence. _____

A stimulus elicits a response.

- - - - - - - - - - - - - - - - - - - - - - - -

**23**

The notation:

$$S \longrightarrow R$$

denotes the elicitation of a response by a stimulus. It is therefore the notation of a(n) _____.

reflex

- - - - - - - - - - - - - - - - - - - - - - - -

**24**

Instead of writing out the definition of a reflex, we can indicate it by the symbolic notation: _____

$$S \longrightarrow R$$

- - - - - - - - - - - - - - - - - - - - - - - -

**25**

The symbolic notation for a relation is called a *paradigm* (pronounced "para-dim" or "para-dime"). The symbols:

$$S \longrightarrow R$$

are a(n) _____ for a(n) _____.

paradigm    reflex

- - - - - - - - - - - - - - - - - - - - - - - -

26

*A stimulus elicits a response.*
WRITE the paradigm for the sentence above.

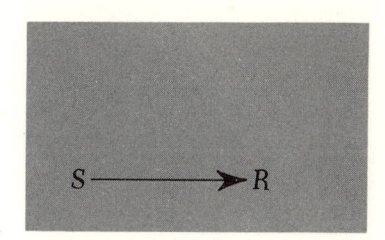

_____

$S \longrightarrow R$

# R-5

## The Principle of Reflex Conditioning (Pavlovian Conditioning)

**1**

In a hungry dog, we can demonstrate the following reflex: *Food in mouth elicits salivation.*

In the paradigm below, FILL IN the parentheses with the names of the stimulus and the response for this reflex:

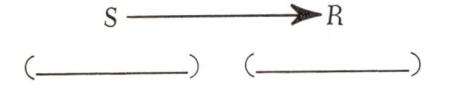

S ────────▶ R
(_____)  (_____)

S ────────▶ R
(food in    (salivation)
mouth)

---

**2**

*Light in eye elicits pupil contraction.*

COMPLETE the paradigm for the reflex above (two letters are required):

_____        _____
(light           (pupil
in eye)          contraction)

S ────────▶ R
(light       (pupil
in eye)      contraction)

---

**3**

*Electric shock applied to the hand elicits increased heart rate.*

DRAW and LABEL the complete paradigm for the reflex above:

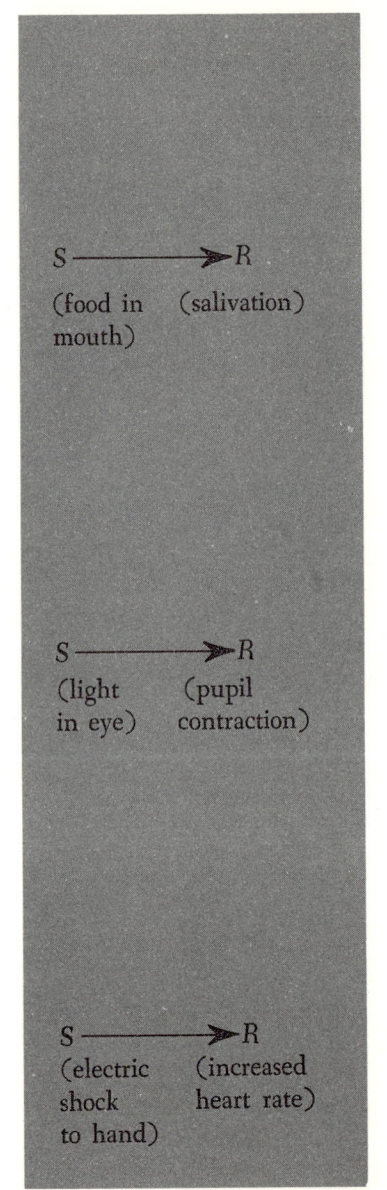

S ────────▶ R
(electric    (increased
shock        heart rate)
to hand)

---

42

**4**

Some stimuli elicit responses without previous learning. DRAW lines from the stimuli to the responses which they elicit:

| Stimuli | Responses |
|---|---|
| food | pupil contraction |
| light | increased heart rate |
| electric shock | salivation |

*Answer:*
food — pupil contraction
light — increased heart rate
electric shock — salivation
(food→salivation, light→pupil contraction, shock→increased heart rate)

---

**5**

A stimulus that elicits a response without previous training is called an *unconditioned stimulus*.

Which do you think is an unconditioned stimulus for the response of salivation?
☐ food in the mouth
☐ a menu

*Answer:* food in the mouth

---

**6**

Other stimuli acquire their power to elicit responses only through training or learning. These are called *conditioned stimuli*.

Which do you think might be a conditioned stimulus for increased heart rate?
☐ the sound of a nearby explosion (dynamite)
☐ the sight of the burning fuse

*Answer:* the sight of the burning fuse

---

**7**

A light in the eye is an unconditioned _____ for pupil contraction.

*Answer:* stimulus

---

**8**

The sound of a dentist's drill might be a(n) _____ stimulus for nausea and trembling.

*Answer:* conditioned

**44 / Reflexes and Conditioned Reflexes**

9

For a Frenchman, a French menu might be a conditioned _____ for a salivary response.

stimulus

---

10

A stimulus that elicits a response without prior training is called a(n) _____ stimulus.

unconditioned

---

11

A reflex prompted by an unconditioned stimulus is called a(n) _____ reflex.

unconditioned

---

12

S ⟶ R is the paradigm for any _____.

reflex

---

13

If S stands for stimulus, then you might guess that the notation for an Unconditioned Stimulus would be _____.

US

---

14

In the paradigm:

　　US ⟶ R

the symbol US stands for _____ _____.
The arrow stands for the word _____.
The R stands for _____.

unconditioned stimulus
elicits
response

---

15

The paradigm:

　　US ⟶ R

designates a(n) _____ reflex.

unconditioned

---

## The Principle of Reflex Conditioning (Pavlovian Conditioning) / 45

16

The paradigm for an unconditioned reflex is

——— ——    ———                      US ⟶ R

---

17

In this paradigm:

US ⟶ R

the arrow signifies the word _____.       elicits

---

18

An unconditioned stimulus is one that will elicit a response without _____.

previous training or learning
(or equivalent answer)

---

19

On the other hand, the ability of some stimuli to elicit responses is conditional (depends) upon some kind of prior training. We have called such stimuli _____ed stimuli.

conditioned

---

20

Stimuli that elicit responses without previous training are called:
- ☐ conditioned stimuli
- ☐ unconditioned stimuli

unconditioned stimuli

---

21

US ⟶ R

Which reflex is an appropriate instance of the paradigm above?
- ☐ photograph elicits blushing
- ☐ rotten food elicits vomiting

rotten food elicits vomiting

---

## 46 / Reflexes and Conditioned Reflexes

**22**

Suppose that we present a puppy with an empty food dish. It is the first time he has ever seen the dish. He looks at the dish. We notice that he does not salivate. Is the dish a US for salivation?

☐ yes
☐ no

> no

- - - - - - - - - - - - - - - - - - - - - - - -

**23**

The stimulus (empty food dish) does not elicit the response without training. In this respect it is initially a:

☐ neutral stimulus
☐ powerful stimulus

> neutral stimulus

- - - - - - - - - - - - - - - - - - - - - - - -

**24**

We know that food in the mouth will produce salivation without previous training. Food in the mouth acts as the _____ stimulus, which is abbreviated _____.

> unconditioned
> US

- - - - - - - - - - - - - - - - - - - - - - - -

**25**

Suppose that we put food in the dish. The puppy looks at the dish and then eats the food.

The dish is a stimulus, and so is the food in the mouth. Which stimulus comes first in time?

☐ the dish
☐ food in the mouth

> the dish

- - - - - - - - - - - - - - - - - - - - - - - -

**26**

After feeding the puppy from the dish a number of times, we notice that when we now put the food dish in front of the puppy he salivates. The dish was once a neutral stimulus. Is it now?

☐ yes
☐ no

> no

- - - - - - - - - - - - - - - - - - - - - - - -

27

FILL IN the terms in the unconditioned reflex just described:

US ———→R
(_____)  (_____)

| US ———→R |
| (food in the mouth)  (salivation) |

What is the neutral stimulus we are pairing with the US? _____

the dish

---

28

The food dish was once a neutral stimulus. But after it has been paired with the US of _____ a number of times, it has acquired the power to elicit a similar _____.

food *or* sight of food

response

---

29

The food dish was a neutral stimulus. We paired it repeatedly with a US for the response of _____.

salivating *or* salivation

---

30

A reflex whose stimulus is a conditioned stimulus is called a *conditioned reflex*. In the conditioned reflex we have just formed in the puppy, the conditioned stimulus is _____ and the response is _____.

the dish *or* sight of dish
salivation

---

31

*Food in the mouth elicits salivation* is a(n):
    ☐ conditioned reflex
    ☐ unconditioned reflex

*Sight of dish elicits salivation* is a(n):
    ☐ conditioned reflex
    ☐ unconditioned reflex

unconditioned reflex

conditioned reflex

---

48 / Reflexes and Conditioned Reflexes

32

The "rule" for producing a conditioned reflex is simple: A previously neutral stimulus is paired with a(n) _____ stimulus. The neutral stimulus then becomes a(n) _____ stimulus.

unconditioned
conditioned

---

33

If the abbreviation for *unconditioned stimulus* is US, you would guess that we abbreviate conditioned stimulus as \_\_\_\_\_.

CS

---

34

NUMBER these events in the proper order:
- a. \_\_\_\_\_ The conditioned stimulus elicits a response.
- b. \_\_\_\_\_ The neutral stimulus does not elicit a response.
- c. \_\_\_\_\_ The neutral stimulus is paired with a US.

Which of the three statements above describes the *procedure* for producing a conditioned reflex? \_\_\_\_\_

a. 3
b. 1
c. 2

c.

---

35

The CS must precede or simultaneously accompany the presentation of the US. Therefore, if we were to present the food first and then the food dish, we (☐ would  ☐ would not) produce a conditioned reflex.

would not

---

36

For successful conditioning, the CS must:

☐ precede or accompany the US

☐ follow the US

precede or accompany the US

---

*The Principle of Reflex Conditioning (Pavlovian Conditioning)* / 49

37

The procedure for producing a conditioned reflex is called *conditioning*.

Conditioning takes place when we pair a neutral stimulus with a(n) _____ _____.

The neutral stimulus then becomes a(n) _____ _____.

unconditioned stimulus *or* US

conditioned stimulus *or* CS

---

38

If a CS and US are not presented simultaneously, which must come first if conditioning is to take place?
- ☐ CS
- ☐ US

CS

---

39

CS ⟶ R

How would you read the paradigm above?
_____

A conditioned stimulus elicits a response. (You could also have said "conditioned reflex.")

---

40

We know that a procedure called conditioning has taken place when a formerly neutral stimulus now _____ the response when presented by itself.

elicits

---

41

The name of the procedure used when we pair a neutral stimulus with a US so that the neutral stimulus becomes a CS is _____.

conditioning

---

42

DESCRIBE in words the procedure for producing a conditioned reflex. _____

> A neutral stimulus is paired with an unconditioned stimulus (or *US*) and becomes a conditioned stimulus (or *CS*). (or equivalent answer)

# R-6

## Forming Conditioned Reflexes

1

Suppose we take a stimulus that initially has no effect (is neutral). After it has been paired with an unconditioned stimulus, the previously neutral stimulus will now be a(n) _____.

conditioned stimulus

---

2

MATCH the following with connecting lines:

the *procedure* ☐    ☐ An originally neutral stimulus is paired with an unconditioned stimulus.

the *result* of ☐    ☐ The neutral stimulus the procedure becomes able to elicit a response.

☐———☐

☐———☐

---

3

We can say that there is a conditioned reflex when a previously neutral stimulus _____ a response similar to the one the *US* elicits.

elicits

---

4

In our descriptions, the term "neutral" refers to the same physical stimulus as the term:
   ☐ CS
   ☐ US

CS

*Before* conditioning, we call it a:
   ☐ CS
   ☐ neutral stimulus

neutral stimulus

*After* conditioning, we call it a:
   ☐ CS
   ☐ neutral stimulus

CS

---

5

The sound of a buzzer does not initially produce pupil contraction. The buzzer is an example of a(n):
- ☐ conditioned stimulus
- ☐ neutral stimulus
- ☐ unconditioned stimulus

neutral stimulus

---

6

A flash of light (stimulus) automatically (without prior training) produces pupil contraction (response). The relationship:

$$US \longrightarrow R$$
(flash of light)  (pupil contraction)

is therefore a(n) _____ _____.

unconditioned reflex

---

7

To make the sound of a buzzer part of a conditioned reflex involving pupil contraction, we could:
- ☐ precede it with a flash of light
- ☐ follow it with a flash of light

follow it with a flash of light

---

8

Before conditioning, the buzzer is a(n) _____ stimulus.

neutral

---

9

The formation of a reflex relation between the buzzer and pupil contraction occurs through the procedure technically known as _____.

conditioning

---

10

In any reflex, a _____ _____ a _____.

stimulus elicits response

**11**

There are two kinds of reflexes: unconditioned and conditioned. When a US elicits a response, which kind is it? _____ _____

| unconditioned reflex

------------------------------

**12**

And when a CS elicits a response, we have a(n) _____ _____.

| conditioned reflex

------------------------------

**13**

$$US \longrightarrow R \quad CS \longrightarrow R$$
$$\quad\; (A) \qquad\qquad (B)$$

*Light in eye elicits pupil contraction.*
This is a(n) _____ reflex and is best illustrated by (☐ paradigm A  ☐ paradigm B).

| unconditioned
| paradigm A

*Sight of food dish elicits salivation.*
This is a(n) _____ reflex and is best illustrated by (☐ paradigm A  ☐ paradigm B).

| conditioned
| paradigm B

------------------------------

**14**

Remember: In order to have any reflex we must have both a(n) _____ and a(n) _____.

| stimulus    response

------------------------------

**15**

In order to build a conditioned reflex, we start off with a stimulus that does not elicit the response and is therefore _____. This stimulus will become the _____ stimulus.

| neutral
| conditioned

------------------------------

**16**

We combine or pair the neutral stimulus with a(n) _____ stimulus.

| unconditioned

------------------------------

**54 / Reflexes and Conditioned Reflexes**

17

When we combine two objects, we have a *pair*. When we combine a neutral S with a *US*, we can speak of _____ the two stimuli.

pairing

- - - - - - - - - - - - - - - - - - - - - - - -

18

The procedure of pairing the neutral stimulus and the *US* causes the neutral stimulus to become a \_\_\_\_.

*CS or* conditioned stimulus

- - - - - - - - - - - - - - - - - - - - - - - -

19

When the CS elicits a response, this relationship is known as a _____ _____.

conditioned reflex

- - - - - - - - - - - - - - - - - - - - - - - -

20

Let's review. We know that food in the mouth elicits salivation.

The relationship:
$$S \longrightarrow R$$
  (food)   (salivation)
is a(n) _____ reflex.

unconditioned

- - - - - - - - - - - - - - - - - - - - - - - -

21

Initially the sight of the food dish does not elicit salivation. Therefore, prior to training, the sight of the food dish is a(n) _____ stimulus.

neutral

- - - - - - - - - - - - - - - - - - - - - - - -

22

If we want to make the sight of the food dish elicit salivation, we pair the sight of the food dish with _____.

food (in the mouth)

- - - - - - - - - - - - - - - - - - - - - - - -

23

After doing so, we find that the sight of the food dish _____ salivation.

elicits

- - - - - - - - - - - - - - - - - - - - - - - -

24

We have produced a(n) _____ reflex.
The CS for this reflex is _____.

| conditioned |
| sight of the food dish |

---

25

A new conditioned reflex is like the original unconditioned reflex, except that one important part has changed. Which statement describes that change?
- ☐ A similar response is now elicited by a different stimulus.
- ☐ A different response is now elicited by the same stimulus.

A similar response is now elicited by a different stimulus.

---

26

Stimulus substitution has taken place.
A(n):
- ☐ conditioned stimulus
- ☐ unconditioned stimulus

has been substituted for a(n):
- ☐ conditioned stimulus
- ☐ unconditioned stimulus

conditioned stimulus

unconditioned stimulus

---

## R-7

## Number of Pairings as an Independent Variable

1

Suppose you owned a puppy. There are many sounds and sights that would accompany his daily feedings (footsteps, cans rattling, getting food dish off floor, etc.). Each of these stimuli would, in time, elicit salivation. These stimuli would play the role of CS in a _____ _____.

conditioned reflex

- - - - - - - - - - - - - - - - - - - - - - - - -

2

These sounds and sights would become CS's through pairing with the US of _____. This pairing procedure is called _____.

food
conditioning

- - - - - - - - - - - - - - - - - - - - - - - - -

3

The conditioning procedure depends upon the _____ of two stimuli.

pairing

- - - - - - - - - - - - - - - - - - - - - - - - -

4

US ⟶ R is the paradigm for a(n) _____ reflex.

unconditioned

- - - - - - - - - - - - - - - - - - - - - - - - -

5

US ⟶ R is the paradigm for condition-
CS ⇢       ing a new reflex.

US stands for the _____.
The arrow is read _____.
CS stands for the _____ _____.
The new reflex is indicated by the dashed line connecting _____ and _____.

unconditioned stimulus
elicits
conditioned stimulus

CS (and) R

- - - - - - - - - - - - - - - - - - - - - - - - -

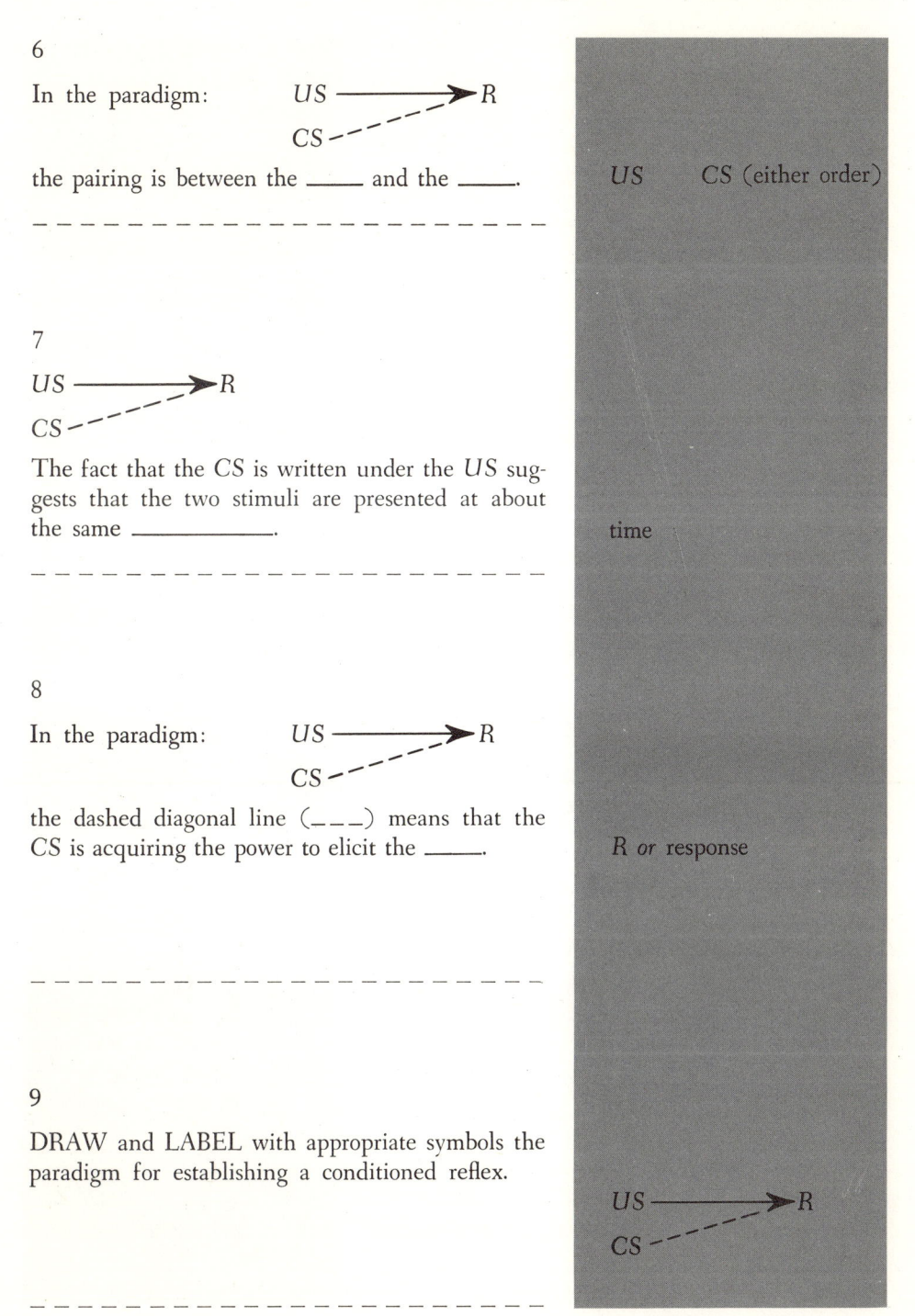

6

In the paradigm:  US ──→ R
                  CS ╌╌╱

the pairing is between the ____ and the ____.   |   US    CS (either order)

---

7

US ──→ R
CS ╌╌╱

The fact that the CS is written under the US suggests that the two stimuli are presented at about the same ____.   |   time

---

8

In the paradigm:  US ──→ R
                  CS ╌╌╱

the dashed diagonal line (╌╌╌) means that the CS is acquiring the power to elicit the ____.   |   R *or* response

---

9

DRAW and LABEL with appropriate symbols the paradigm for establishing a conditioned reflex.

US ──→ R
CS ╌╌╱

58 / Reflexes and Conditioned Reflexes

10
If a puppy salivates upon seeing an empty food dish, the conditioning procedure could be shown as:

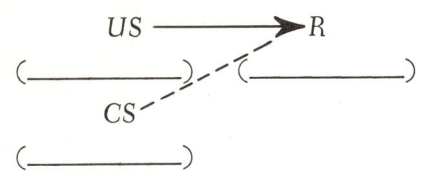

US ────────► R
(_____)-(_____)
       CS
       (_____)

US = food in mouth
CS = empty food dish

R = salivation

---

11
Once the CS elicits the response, we have a _____ reflex.

conditioned

---

12
DRAW a paradigm for the conditioned reflex by showing the conditioned stimulus eliciting the response. The line which was dashed in the diagram of the procedure should now be solid, since the new reflex is formed; it should be horizontal instead of diagonal; and since it is now eliciting the response, an arrow should be added.

CS ────────► R

---

13
US ────────► R     CS ────────► R
CS ─ ─ ─
   (A)              (B)

Which of the two paradigms above shows the pairing procedure? _____

Shows a conditioned reflex after conditioning is complete? _____

Incorporates an unconditioned reflex? _____

Must be carried out before the other paradigm can be attained? _____

Shows a "new" stimulus eliciting an "old" response? _____

A

B

A

A

B

---

## 14

A college student proposed to demonstrate conditioning by learning to control his own heart rate. The procedure he devised involved pairing a pistol shot with the spoken word *palpitate*. The pistol shot initially produced a rapid heart rate, and therefore was the _____.

unconditioned stimulus *or US*

---

## 15

The word *palpitate* does not normally cause increased heart rate. It is therefore a neutral stimulus, which the student hoped to turn into a(n) _____.

conditioned stimulus *or CS*

---

## 16

Now, if the word *palpitate* is said just before a pistol shot, we are pairing the two. COMPLETE the paradigm below:

US ⟶ R
(shot)   (rapid heart rate)

___ ___
(_____)

CS
(palpitate)

---

## 17

With repeated pairing, the word *palpitate* alone will _____ rapid heart rate.

DRAW and LABEL a paradigm for the completed conditioned reflex.

elicit

CS ⟶ R
(palpitate) (rapid heart rate)

60 / Reflexes and Conditioned Reflexes

18

(Look at Panel R-7-1.)

Let us now examine some laboratory studies that illustrate precise control and accurate observation of the conditioning process.

(READ THROUGH PANEL R-7-1. You will refer to this panel for frames 19 through 42.)

Pavlov's experiment was concerned with the conditioning of the _____ reflex.

salivary

The organism used as an experimental subject was a _____.

dog

------

19

(Refer to Panel R-7-1.)

In this experiment, identify the:

    1. R _____

1. salivation *or* drops of saliva
 (or equivalent answer)

    2. CS _____

2. sound of the metronome

    3. US _____

3. food in the dog's mouth

------

20

(Refer to Panel R-7-1.)

Session I demonstrated the:
- ☐ conditioned reflex
- ☐ unconditioned reflex

unconditioned reflex

------

21

(Refer to Panel R-7-1.)

DRAW and LABEL the paradigm for the unconditioned reflex in Pavlov's experiment.

US ⟶ R
(food in mouth)  (salivation)

------

22

(Refer to Panel R-7-1.)
What was the latency of the salivation response to the food stimulus? _____    2 seconds

---

23

(Refer to Panel R-7-1.)
Are *US* and *CS* paired in Session II?
    ☐ yes
    ☐ no    no

---

24

(Refer to Panel R-7-1.)
What could you do to demonstrate that the metronome was originally a neutral stimulus? _____    present the metronome without the food

Did Pavlov do this? ☐ yes ☐ no    yes
Did the response occur? ☐ yes ☐ no    no

---

25

(Refer to Panel R-7-1.)
In which session did the actual conditioning take place? _____    Session III

---

26

(Refer to Panel R-7-1.)
What are the two stimuli that are paired in Session III? (NAME the specific stimuli.)
_____
_____    food in mouth
sound of metronome
(either order)

62 / Reflexes and Conditioned Reflexes

27

**(Refer to Panel R-7-1.)**

What time interval elapsed between presentation of the CS and the US? _____

5 seconds

---

28

**(Refer to Panel R-7-1.)**

DRAW the paradigm for the first trial of Session III. Again, LABEL the actual experimental stimuli and response. (*Don't forget the dotted line!*)

US ⟶ R
(food in    ⟋ (salivation)
mouth) ⟋
  CS ⟋
(sound of
metronome)

---

29

**(Refer to Panel R-7-1.)**

How many times were CS and US paired in Pavlov's experiment? _____

10 times

---

30

**(Refer to Panel R-7-1.)**

Each pairing in the experiment is called a *trial*. Measures of the conditioned reflex were obtained at Trial No. ____ and Trial No. ____.

5      10

---

31

**(Refer to Panel R-7-1.)**

How would you draw the paradigm of the new reflex that has been established? LABEL the actual stimulus and response.

CS ⟶ R
(sound of    (salivation)
metronome)

---

32

(Refer to Panel R-7-1.)

The metronome in Session II was shown to be a neutral stimulus because when it was sounded _____.

no salivation occurred (or equivalent answer)

In Session III, the neutral stimulus became a _____.

CS

------------------------------

33

(Refer to Panel R-7-1.)

Pavlov used two measures of the response that we have seen before: latency and magnitude.

Latency was measured in:
    ☐ drops of saliva
    ☐ seconds

seconds

Magnitude was measured in:
    ☐ drops of saliva
    ☐ seconds

drops of saliva

------------------------------

34

(Refer to Panel R-7-1.)

The latency, to be more precise, was the time, in seconds, from the beginning of a stimulus to the beginning of a(n) _____.

R (salivation)

------------------------------

64 / Reflexes and Conditioned Reflexes

35

(Refer to Panel R-7-1.)

Let us examine changes in the magnitude of the response.

In Session I, the US was presented alone, and response magnitude was _____ drops of saliva.

15

In Session II, before any pairings, the metronome was a neutral stimulus, and elicited _____ drops.

0

In Session III, after five pairings of metronome and food, the CS elicited _____ drops.

3

After ten pairings, the CS elicited _____ drops.

10

------

36

(Refer to Panel R-7-1.)

```
US ─────▶ R
(food)    ╱ (salivation)
        ╱
CS ╱
(metronome)
```

Repeated pairings in the conditioning procedure above have the following effect upon the conditioned reflex:

What happens to the magnitude of the response to the CS? _____

It increases *or* gets larger.

------

37

(Refer to Panel R-7-1.)

Now let us examine changes in the latency.

In Session I, the US was presented alone, and response latency was _____ seconds.

2

In Session II, the metronome elicited no response. Could a latency be measured?

☐ yes
☐ no

no

In Session III, after five pairings of metronome and food, the latency to the CS was _____ seconds.

4

After ten pairings, the latency was _____ seconds.

2

------

38

(Refer to Panel R-7-1.)

$$US \longrightarrow R$$
(food)  (salivation)
$$CS$$
(metronome)

What effect do repeated pairings in the conditioning procedure have upon the latency of the response to the CS? _____

The latency decreases *or* gets smaller.

---

39

(Refer to Panel R-7-1.)

The procedure for conditioning consists in pairings of a _____ with a _____.

The result of this procedure is a new reflex:

$$CS \longrightarrow R$$

The results of repeated pairings upon this new reflex are that:

   Response magnitude _____.
   Latency _____.

CS    US
(either order)

increases *or* gets larger
decreases *or* gets smaller

---

40

(Refer to Panel R-7-1.)
You will remember that response latency and response magnitude are both examples of:
   ☐ dependent variables
   ☐ independent variables

dependent variables

---

66 / Reflexes and Conditioned Reflexes

41  (Refer to Panel R-7-1.)

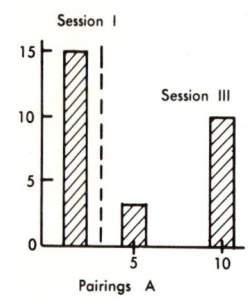

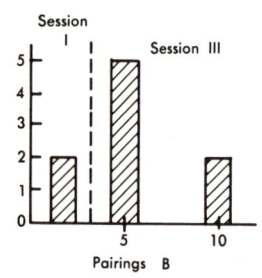

Graph A shows the changes in one dependent variable measured by Pavlov. Which one is it? _____

The values on the vertical axis represent _____.

Graph B shows the changes in the second dependent variable measured by Pavlov. Which one is it? _____

The values on the vertical axis represent _____.

magnitude

drops (of saliva)

latency

seconds (time in seconds)

- - - - - - - - - - - - - - - - - - - - - - - -

42

Latency and magnitude are both dependent variables that describe aspects of:

☐ responses, or parts of behavior

☐ stimuli, or parts of the environment

responses, or parts of behavior

- - - - - - - - - - - - - - - - - - - - - - - -

43

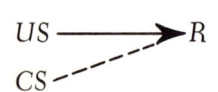

US ———▶ R
CS - - -↗

As conditioning progresses, these variables change. To test the new reflex, we present the _____ alone, and find that the _____ of the response increases, while its _____ decreases.

CS
magnitude
latency

- - - - - - - - - - - - - - - - - - - - - - - -

44

When a dependent variable changes value, we look for the independent variable that accounts for the change. In Pavlov's experiment, was the intensity of the US changed?
- ☐ yes
- ☐ no                                                         no

Was the intensity of the CS changed?
- ☐ yes
- ☐ no                                                         no

Was the number of pairings of the CS and the US changed?
- ☐ yes                                                        yes
- ☐ no

------------------------------------------------

45

The variable that the experimenter manipulates directly is the:
- ☐ dependent variable
- ☐ independent variable                       independent variable

In Pavlov's experiment, the experimenter directly manipulated:
- ☐ latency and magnitude
- ☐ the number of pairings                     the number of pairings

------------------------------------------------

46

The number of pairings of CS and US is a(n) _____ variable.                      independent

The resulting change in response latency in the conditioned reflex is a(n) _____ variable.     dependent

The resulting change in response magnitude in the conditioned reflex is a(n) _____ variable.   dependent

------------------------------------------------

**47**

With an increased number of pairings, the latency of salivation:
- ☐ increases
- ☐ decreases

    decreases

---

**48**

Latency of salivation and number of stimulus pairings are:
- ☐ directly related
- ☐ inversely related

    inversely related

Magnitude of salivation and number of stimulus pairings are:
- ☐ directly related
- ☐ inversely related

    directly related

---

**49**

(Look at Panel R-7-2.)

In Anrep's study, biscuit powder in the mouth was the _____.

    US

The originally neutral stimulus, which became a CS when paired with the biscuit powder, was a _____.

    tone (of 637.5 cycles per second)

---

**50**

(Refer to Panel R-7-2.)

During conditioning, the CS lasted for _____ seconds.

    5

The US was presented _____ seconds later.

    2 or 3

Thus:
- ☐ the CS preceded the US
- ☐ the US preceded the CS

    the CS preceded the US

---

## Number of Pairings as an Independent Variable / 69

**51**

(Refer to Panel R-7-2.)

DRAW and LABEL a paradigm of the conditioning procedure in Anrep's experiment.

US ⟶ R
(biscuit        (salivation)
powder)
CS
(tone)

---

**52**

(Refer to Panel R-7-2.)

At irregular intervals of 5 to 35 minutes, the experimenter repeatedly _____ the CS with the US.

paired

---

**53**

(Refer to Panel R-7-2.)

The experiment lasted 16 days, and over this period the total number of pairings was _____.

50

The progress of the conditioned reflex was tested by presenting the _____ alone.

CS or tone

This testing occurred _____ times.

6

---

**54**

(Refer to Panel R-7-2.)

US ⟶ R      CS ⟶ R
CS
   (A)         (B)

Which paradigm represents the pairing procedure, repeated 50 times? _____

A

Which paradigm represents the testing procedure, repeated 6 times? _____

B

---

70 / Reflexes and Conditioned Reflexes

55

(Refer to Panel R-7-2.)

The dependent variables were:
_____ of the response, which was measured in _____ of _____; _____ of the response, which was measured in _____.

| | |
|---|---|
| magnitude | |
| drops (of) saliva | latency |
| seconds | |

- - - - - - - - - - - - - - - - - - - - - -

56

(Refer to Panel R-7-2.)

Did one pairing establish a conditioned reflex in this experiment?
☐ yes
☐ no

After 30 pairings, response magnitude was \_\_\_\_ drops, and the latency was \_\_\_\_ seconds.

no
60
2

- - - - - - - - - - - - - - - - - - - - - -

57

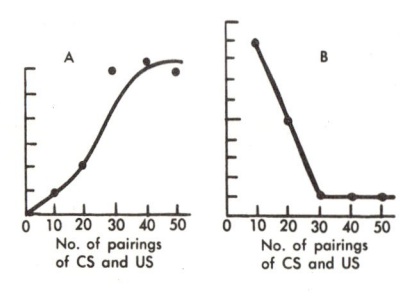

Graph A shows the effects of conditioning upon the _____ of the response.

Graph B shows the effects of conditioning upon the _____ of the response.

magnitude

latency

- - - - - - - - - - - - - - - - - - - - - -

58

MATCH the following:

    *a.* the scientist who first studied conditioned reflexes    1. ____dog

    *b.* the favorite subject used in studies of conditioned reflexes    2. ____Ivan Pavlov

    *c.* the response often used in studies of conditioned reflexes    3. ____salivation

1. *b.*

2. *a.*

3. *c.*

---

59

The kind of conditioning described in this section has come to be named for the man who first studied it. Hence it is known as Pavlovian conditioning. Every case of Pavlovian conditioning involves at least ____ (how many) stimuli.

2

---

60

DRAW and LABEL the paradigm for the unconditioned reflex used by Pavlov and Anrep.

US ⟶ R
(food)      (salivation)

---

61

The formation of a new conditioned reflex is the result of ____ conditioning.

This is accomplished by the ____ of a CS and a US.

Typically, the ____ precedes the ____ by a few seconds.

Pavlovian

pairing

CS     US

---

## 62

The result of such pairings is that the CS comes to _____ the R.

As the new reflex gets stronger:
    response magnitude _____;
    response latency _____.

*elicit*

*increases or gets larger*
*decreases or gets shorter*

---

## 63

In Pavlovian conditioning, large magnitudes and short latencies are produced by:
    ☐ few pairings of CS and US
    ☐ many pairings of CS and US

*many pairings of CS and US*

---

## 64

SKETCH the general trend in the magnitude and the latency as repeated pairings of CS and US established a conditioned reflex:

Magnitude | No. of pairings

Latency | No. of pairings

---

## 65

In Pavlovian conditioning, magnitude and latency are commonly used (☐ dependent ☐ independent) variables.

*dependent*

---

## 66

The independent variable in Anrep's experiment was _____.

*the number of pairings (of CS and US)*

# R-8

## Temporal Patterns in Conditioning

**1**

PREVIEW FRAME

Any given stimulus may last a short time or a long time. When two stimuli are paired, as in conditioning, the time relations between them may affect the conditioning process. This set will take up these questions in some detail.

NO RESPONSE REQUIRED

> NO RESPONSE REQUIRED; GO ON TO NEXT FRAME.

---

**2**

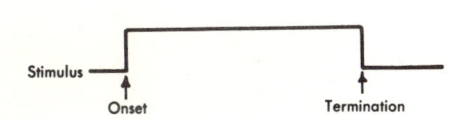

The diagram above represents the presentation of a single stimulus. The horizontal line jogs upward with the _____ of the stimulus, and back down again with its _____.

> onset
> termination

74 / Reflexes and Conditioned Reflexes

3

$S_1$ and $S_2$ have the same onset. Which one terminates later? ____   $S_2$
Which one has the greater duration? ____   $S_2$

---

4

Which stimulus has the earlier onset? ____   $S_1$
Which stimulus terminates first? ____   $S_2$
Which has the greater duration? ____   $S_1$

---

5

In this diagrammatic representation, the onset of the stimulus is labelled:
- ☐ A
- ☐ B
- ☐ C

B

The termination of the stimulus is labelled:
- ☐ A
- ☐ B
- ☐ C

C

---

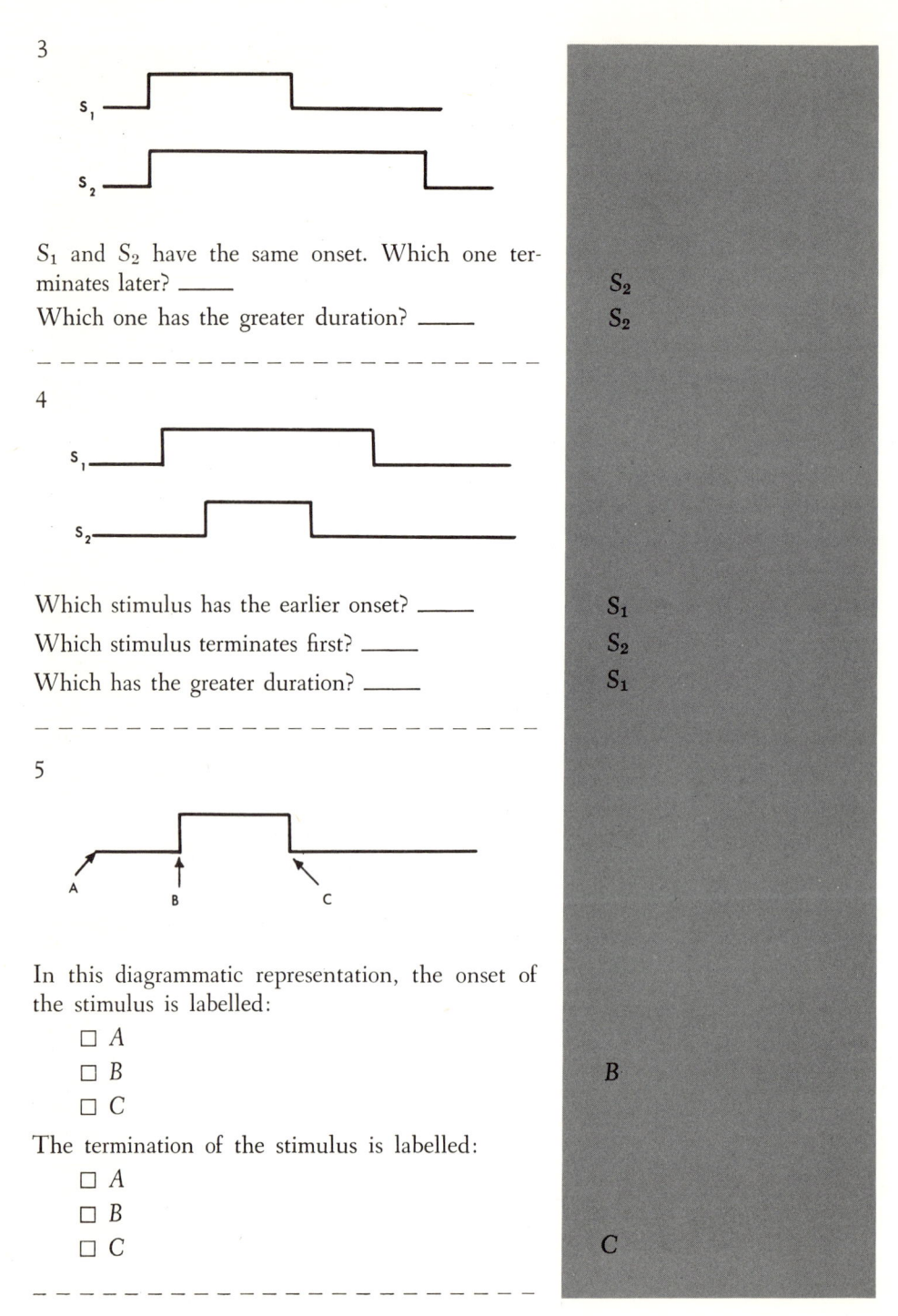

6

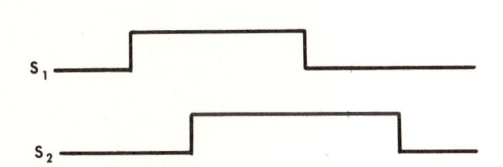

Here are two stimuli. Each has an onset and a termination. COMPLETE the list of the four events in the temporal order shown in the diagram:
First: the onset of $S_1$.

Second: the _____ of _____.

Third: the _____ of _____.

Fourth: the _____ of _____.

(First: the onset of $S_1$.)

Second: the onset of $S_2$

Third: the termination of $S_1$.

Fourth: the termination of $S_2$.

---

7

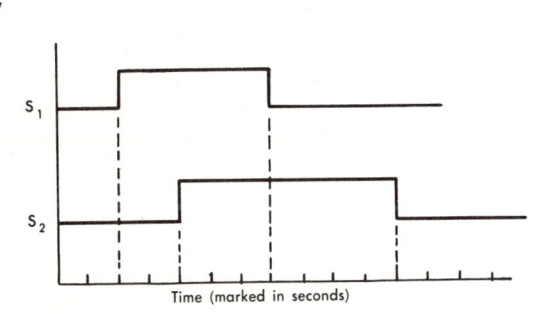

Time (marked in seconds)

The duration of $S_1$ is _____ seconds.
The onset of $S_2$ follows the onset of $S_1$ by _____ seconds.
Thus, the two stimuli *overlap* during the last _____ seconds of $S_1$.
What is the duration of $S_2$? _____ seconds.
How long does $S_2$ persist after $S_1$ is terminated? _____ seconds.
Thus, the two stimuli overlap during the first _____ seconds of $S_2$.

5

2

3

7

4

3

8

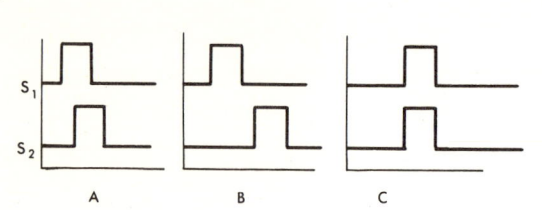

$S_1$ and $S_2$ are two stimuli of equal duration. In the blank following each descriptive sentence below, WRITE the letter of the diagram that the sentence describes:

The amount of overlap between $S_1$ and $S_2$ is greatest when their onsets and terminations are simultaneous. _____   C

There is some overlap when the onset of $S_1$ precedes the onset of $S_2$, but the onset of $S_2$ precedes the termination of $S_1$. _____   A

There is no overlap when the termination of $S_1$ precedes the onset of $S_2$. _____   B

- - - - - - - - - - - - - - - - - - - - - - - -

9

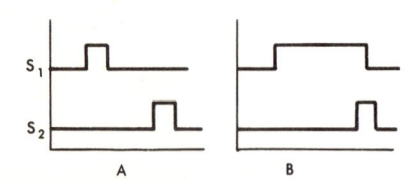

Which case—A or B—most closely resembles the time relations when:

the smell of food precedes tasting it? _____   B

the cocking of a pistol precedes the noise of its firing? _____   A

a flash of distant lightning precedes the sound of thunder? _____   A

the whine of an artillery shell precedes the sound of its explosion? _____   B

10

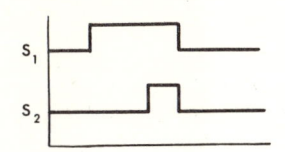

The relation between any two stimuli can be diagrammed as we have been doing. But we are interested in cases in which one of the stimuli is an unconditioned stimulus. The diagram above resembles the pairing procedure employed by Pavlov and Anrep. Which stimulus in the picture is the US? _____

$S_2$

---

11

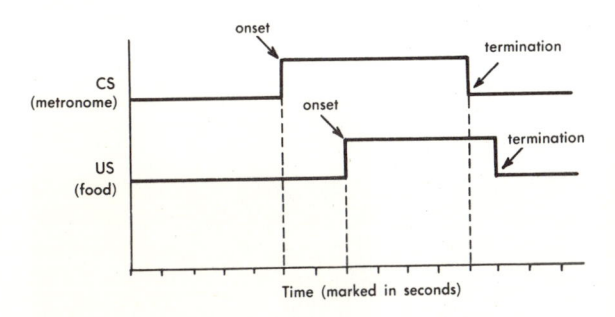

The figure above shows graphically a conditioning procedure that is commonly employed.

The onset of the CS precedes the onset of the US by _____ seconds.

The CS and the US overlap for _____ seconds.

2

4

78 / Reflexes and Conditioned Reflexes

12

This procedure, in which the CS precedes the US by a short interval and the CS overlaps the US in time, is known as *simultaneous* conditioning.

Which of these two diagrams represents *simultaneous conditioning*? (CHECK ONE.)

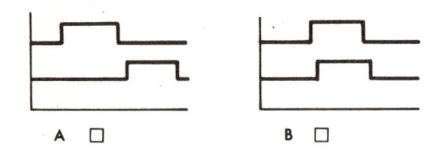

A ☐   B ☐

*B*

---

13

A procedure for pairing CS and US is called *simultaneous*:

1. if the CS and the US begin at the same instant. This is the case in diagram _____.

    *A*

    or

2. if the CS precedes the US only by a short interval. This is the case in diagram _____.

    *B*

    and

3. whether the CS precedes the US or not, the two stimuli have some overlap in time. This is the case in both _____ and _____.

    *A* (and) *B*

The one case above that is *not* an example of simultaneous pairing is _____.

*C*

---

26

*A stimulus elicits a response.*
WRITE the paradigm for the sentence above.

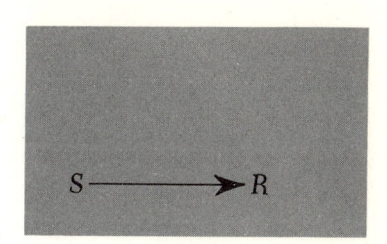

_____

-------------------------

S⟶R

# R-5

## The Principle of Reflex Conditioning (Pavlovian Conditioning)

**1**

In a hungry dog, we can demonstrate the following reflex: *Food in mouth elicits salivation.*

In the paradigm below, FILL IN the parentheses with the names of the stimulus and the response for this reflex:

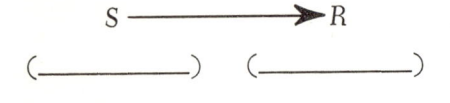

S ──────▶ R
(_____)  (_____)

> S ──────▶ R
> (food in   (salivation)
> mouth)

---

**2**

> *Light in eye elicits pupil contraction.*

COMPLETE the paradigm for the reflex above (two letters are required):

_____        _____
(light             (pupil
in eye)            contraction)

> S ──────▶ R
> (light     (pupil
> in eye)    contraction)

---

**3**

> *Electric shock applied to the hand elicits increased heart rate.*

DRAW and LABEL the complete paradigm for the reflex above:

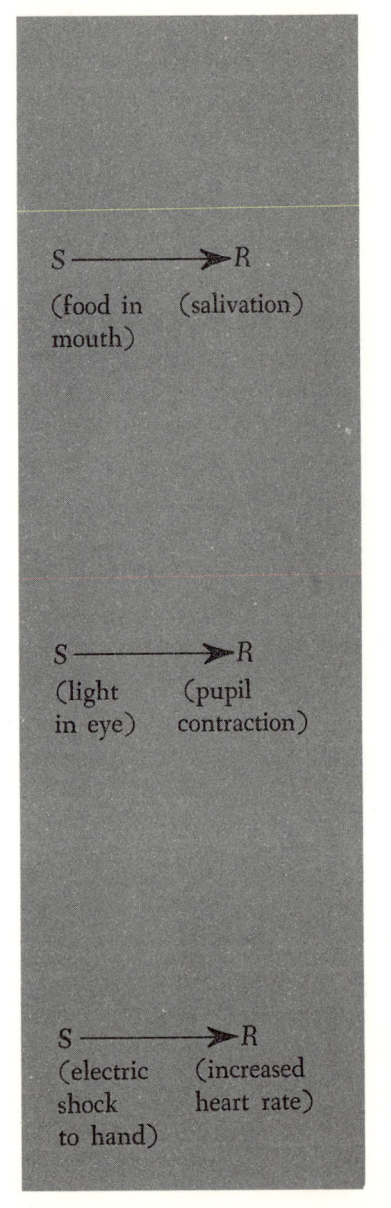

> S ──────▶ R
> (electric   (increased
> shock       heart rate)
> to hand)

---

42

**20**

Simultaneous conditioning can be defined as a conditioning procedure in which:

    *a.* The CS _____ the US by 5 seconds or less.

    *b.* The CS and US _____.

precedes

overlap

------

**21**

To test whether the conditioning procedure has been *successful*, we would present the CS alone and observe whether the _____ occurs.

response

------

**22**

Pavlov and other workers have found simultaneous conditioning to be a powerful pairing procedure. This means that the formation of conditioned reflexes is (☐ difficult   ☐ easy) when using this procedure.

easy

------

**23**

They have also found conditioning to be most effective when the CS precedes the US by an interval of about one-fourth of a second to two seconds. Does this fall within the definition of simultaneous conditioning?

    ☐ yes
    ☐ no

Thus, if CS and US are *strictly* simultaneous, conditioning is (☐ less effective   ☐ more effective) than when the CS precedes the US by a short interval.

yes

less effective

------

82 / Reflexes and Conditioned Reflexes

24

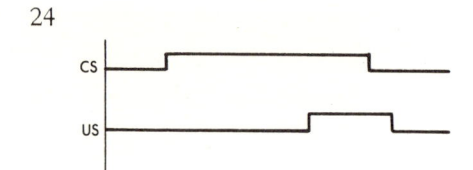

LOOK at the diagrammed procedure above.
Does the CS overlap the US? ☐ yes ☐ no
Does the CS precede the US? ☐ yes ☐ no
If it does, by how many seconds? _____

yes
yes
7

---

25

In terms of our definition, does the CS precede the US by a long interval or a short interval? _____

by a long interval

26

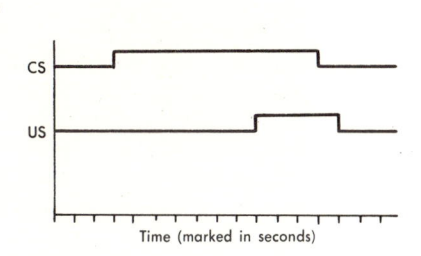

For simultaneous conditioning:
    *a.* The CS must _____ the US by \_\_\_\_ seconds or less.

    *b.* The CS and the US must _____ in time.

Does the procedure illustrated in the diagram satisfy both of these criteria for simultaneous conditioning?

    ☐ yes  ☐ no

CIRCLE the statement letter(s) above that the diagrammed procedure satisfies.

precede
5
overlap

no
You should have circled *b.*

------

27

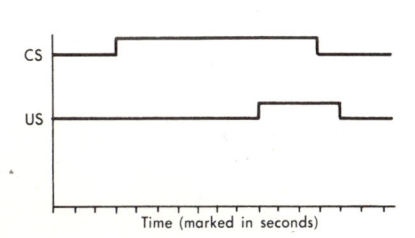

This diagram does not picture the procedure of simultaneous conditioning. Why not? _____

because the CS begins more than 5 seconds before the US
(or equivalent answer)

------

## 28

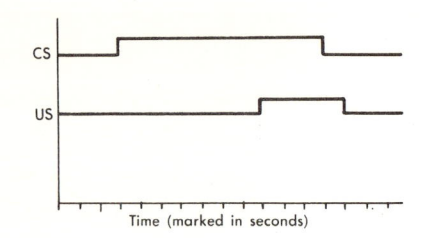

This procedure is known as *delayed conditioning*. In what two ways is it like simultaneous conditioning?

    a. _____

    b. _____

*a.* The CS precedes the US.
*b.* The CS overlaps the US.

---

## 29

Delayed conditioning is unlike simultaneous conditioning in that the CS precedes the US by _____.

*more than* 5 seconds

---

## 30

If the CS begins a "long" time before the US and overlaps it, we speak of _____ conditioning.

delayed

---

## 31

DEFINE delayed conditioning:
    a. The CS precedes the US by _____.

a long interval (an interval longer than 5 seconds)

    b. The CS and the US _____.

overlap
(or equivalent answers)

**32**

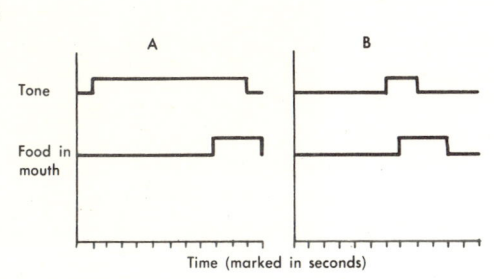

Which illustration represents simultaneous conditioning? \_\_\_\_\_
The other diagram illustrates _____.

B
delayed conditioning

---

**33**

Pavlov and other workers found that conditioning could be carried out by the delayed pairing procedure. They found it harder to do, and less effective, than _____ conditioning.

simultaneous

---

**34**

Delayed conditioning becomes more difficult as the interval between the CS and the US becomes _____.

greater *or* longer

---

**35**

At the very beginning of a delayed conditioning experiment, the CS (initially a neutral stimulus) is presented, say for 15 seconds. At the end of 15 seconds, we present the \_\_\_\_\_.
The US elicits the _____.

US
response

## 86 / Reflexes and Conditioned Reflexes

**36**

At the beginning of the experiment, the response would be elicited by the US and appear in position _____ (letter).

After a number of pairings, the CS will elicit the response with a *short* latency, and the response would appear in position _____.

However, after a very large number of pairings with the same delay interval, the response occurs with a longer latency to the CS but still prior to the US. Therefore, R will occur in position _____.

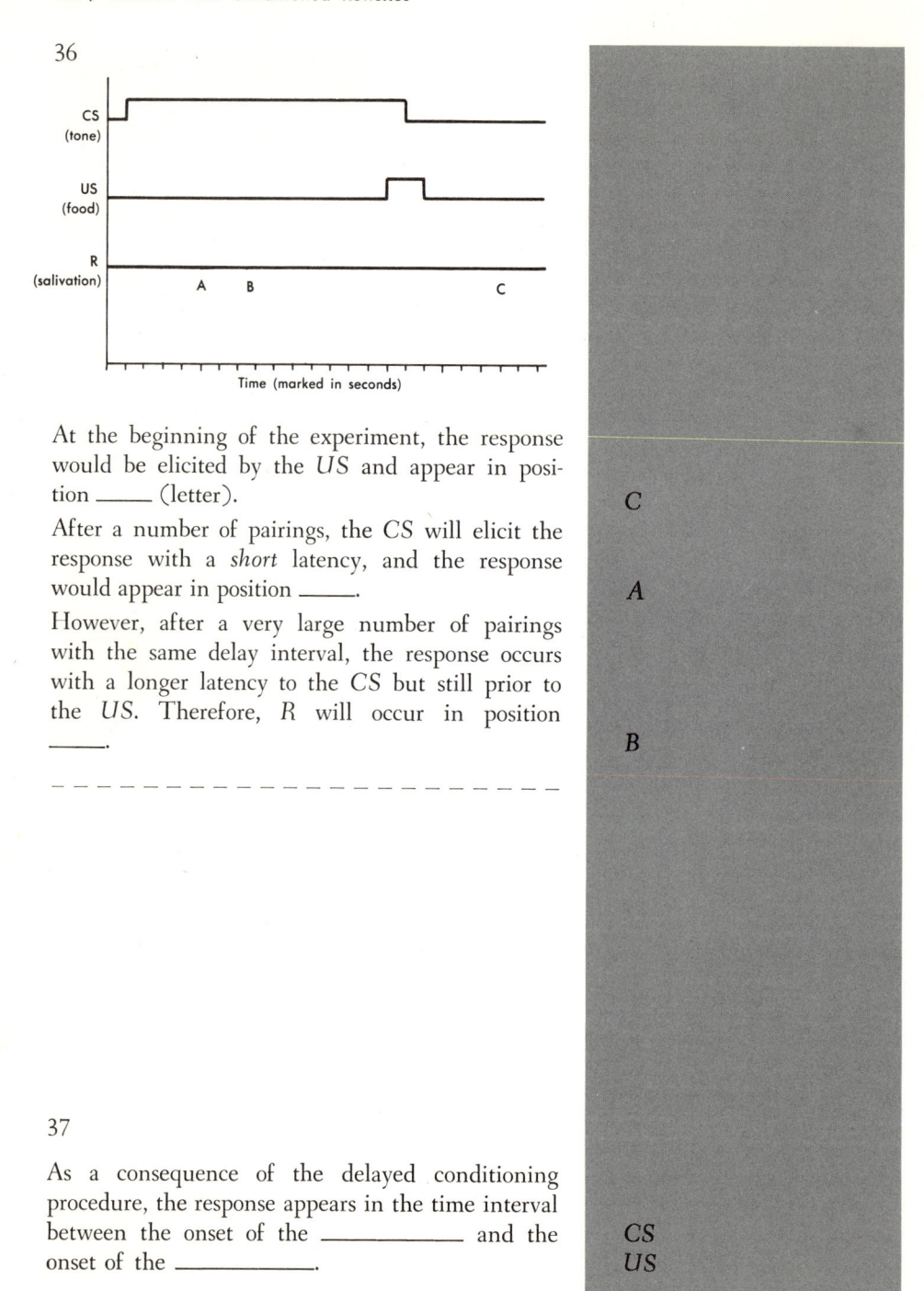

------

**37**

As a consequence of the delayed conditioning procedure, the response appears in the time interval between the onset of the _____ and the onset of the _____.

------

C

A

B

CS
US

38

Early in conditioning, as the CS acquires the power to elicit the response, the response begins to appear:
- ☐ soon after the CS is presented
- ☐ just before the US is presented

But after prolonged exposure to the delayed conditioning procedure, the response appears:
- ☐ soon after the CS is presented
- ☐ with a longer latency to the CS, but prior to the US

*soon after the CS is presented*

*with a longer latency to the CS, but prior to the US*

---

39

On the first conditioning trial (i.e., the first pairing) when the CS is presented, the response:
- ☐ occurs
- ☐ does not occur

*does not occur*

---

40

In early trials using the delayed conditioning procedure, the response occurs (☐ early  ☐ late) in the CS interval.

*early*

---

41

With prolonged training using delayed conditioning, the response occurs (☐ closer to  ☐ farther from) the US.

*closer to*

---

42

So, as delayed conditioning proceeds, the latency of the response to the CS is initially (☐ long  ☐ short) and later becomes (☐ longer  ☐ shorter).

*short   longer*

---

88 / Reflexes and Conditioned Reflexes

43

With prolonged delayed conditioning, the latency of the response to the CS still remains shorter than the interval between the CS and the _____.

*US*

---

44

We have discussed two conditioning procedures. They are called _____ conditioning and _____ conditioning.

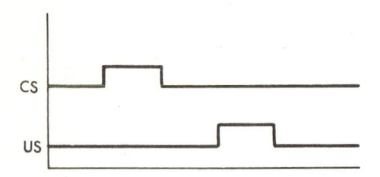

*simultaneous*
*delayed*
*(either order)*

Does this diagram fit the definition of either of these two procedures?

☐ yes
☐ no

*no*

---

45

Here is an illustration of *trace conditioning*:

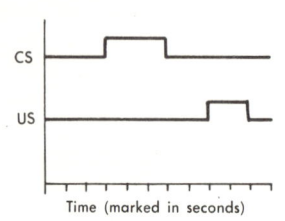

Do the two stimuli ever overlap in trace conditioning?

☐ yes
☐ no

*no*

This procedure is different from simultaneous or delayed conditioning because the CS termination:

☐ precedes the US onset
☐ follows the US onset

*precedes the US onset*

---

46

In trace conditioning, the CS and the US:
- ☐ must overlap
- ☐ must not overlap

must not overlap

---

47

Which of the following statements is an example of the procedure for trace conditioning?
- ☐ The smell of food precedes its taste.
- ☐ The click of cocking a pistol precedes the sound of its firing.

The click of cocking a pistol precedes the sound of its firing.

---

48

When the CS precedes but does *not* overlap the US, we speak of _____ conditioning.

trace

---

49

DESCRIBE the trace conditioning procedure.
_____

In trace conditioning, the CS precedes the US and does not overlap the US.

---

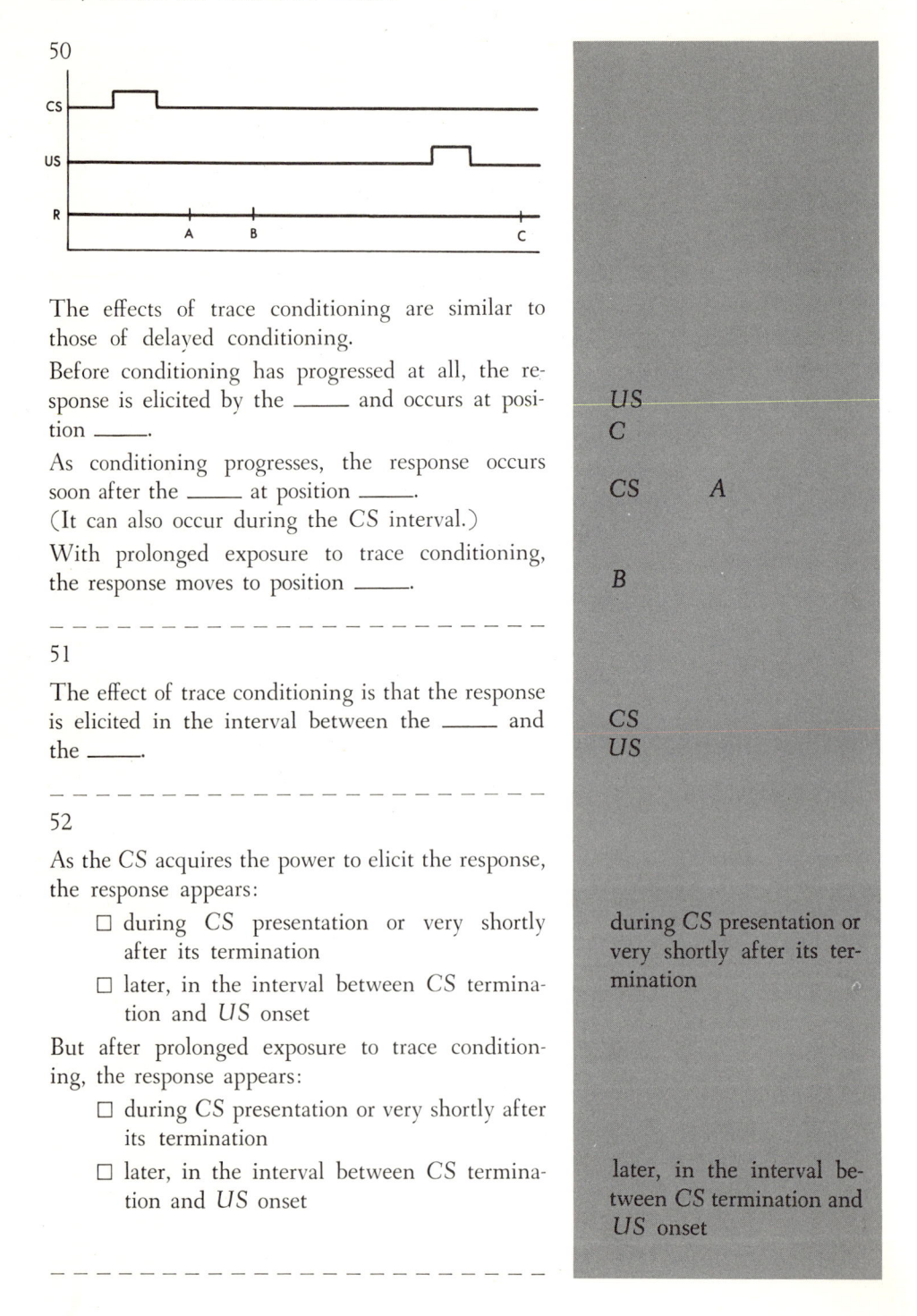

The effects of trace conditioning are similar to those of delayed conditioning.

Before conditioning has progressed at all, the response is elicited by the _____ and occurs at position _____.

*US*
*C*

As conditioning progresses, the response occurs soon after the _____ at position _____.
(It can also occur during the CS interval.)

*CS    A*

With prolonged exposure to trace conditioning, the response moves to position _____.

*B*

- - - - - - - - - - - - - - - - - - - - - - - -

51

The effect of trace conditioning is that the response is elicited in the interval between the _____ and the _____.

*CS*
*US*

- - - - - - - - - - - - - - - - - - - - - - - -

52

As the CS acquires the power to elicit the response, the response appears:

☐ during CS presentation or very shortly after its termination

☐ later, in the interval between CS termination and US onset

during CS presentation or very shortly after its termination

But after prolonged exposure to trace conditioning, the response appears:

☐ during CS presentation or very shortly after its termination

☐ later, in the interval between CS termination and US onset

later, in the interval between CS termination and US onset

- - - - - - - - - - - - - - - - - - - - - - - -

**53**

So, as trace conditioning proceeds, the latency of the response to the CS first is (☐ long  ☐ short), and later becomes (☐ longer  ☐ shorter).

short
longer

---

**54**

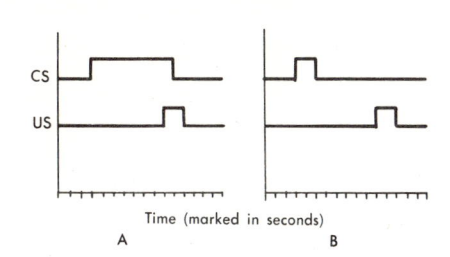

Time (marked in seconds)
A          B

Procedure A shows _____ conditioning.
Procedure B shows _____ conditioning.

delay *or* delayed
trace

---

**55**

Delay          Trace

In which procedure does the response come to occur at a time when no stimulus is present?
_____

in trace conditioning

---

## 56

With which procedure would it be *most* difficult to produce Pavlovian conditioning? _____

trace conditioning

---

## 57

Pavlov found trace conditioning to be the most difficult to obtain.

The next most difficult procedure was _____ conditioning.

The easiest procedure was _____ conditioning.

delayed

simultaneous

---

## 58

What is the most effective temporal arrangement of stimuli for producing conditioning?

- ☐ strictly simultaneous presentation of CS and US
- ☐ CS precedes the US by ¼ second to 2 seconds and overlaps the US
- ☐ CS precedes but does not overlap the US

CS precedes the US by ¼ second to 2 seconds and overlaps the US

---

59

Each of the diagrams below represents a stage in the training of an animal using trace conditioning procedures. The order of the diagrams is rearranged.

(A)

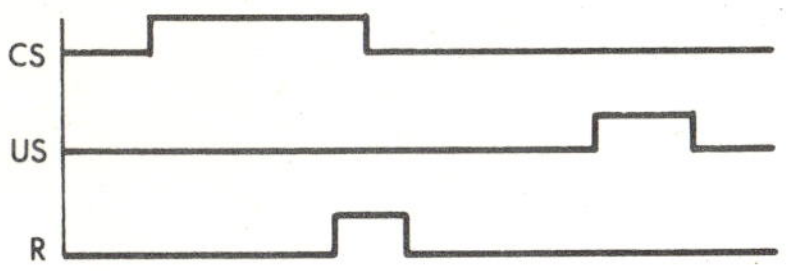
CS
US
R

(B)

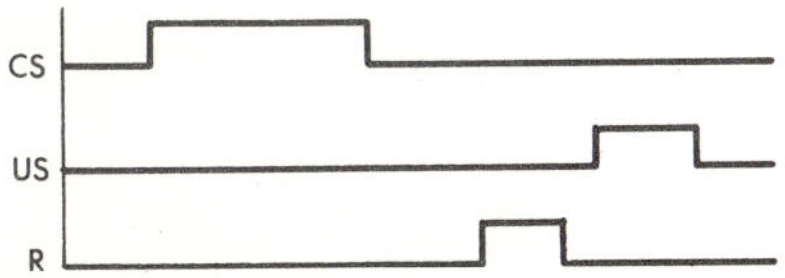
CS
US
R

(C)

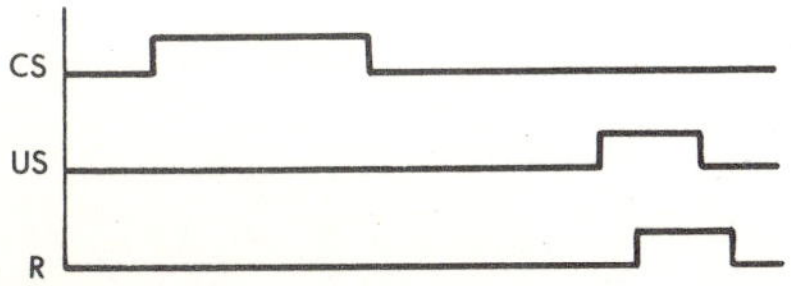
CS
US
R

Which diagram represents:

an early stage in trace conditioning? ____

a later stage in trace conditioning? ____

the latest stage in trace conditioning? ____

C
A
B

60

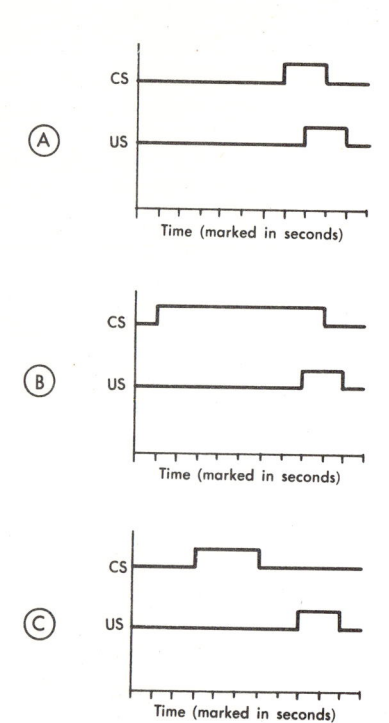

[Illustration A: CS pulse followed by US pulse, non-overlapping]

[Illustration B: CS onset early, sustained through US pulse, ending together]

[Illustration C: CS pulse ends before US pulse begins]

Illustration *A* represents the procedure for _____ conditioning.

Illustration *B* represents the procedure for _____ conditioning.

Illustration *C* represents the procedure for _____ conditioning.

- - - - - - - - - - - - - - - - - - - - - -

simultaneous

delayed

trace

# R-9

## Higher Order Conditioning

READ THROUGH PANEL R-9-1 BEFORE GOING ON TO THE FIRST ITEM.

---

1

(Refer to Panel R-9-1, paragraph 1.)

The *US* in initial conditioning is _____.

food in the mouth

---

2

(Refer to Panel R-9-1, paragraph 1.)

The original *CS* is a _____.

light

---

3

(Refer to Panel R-9-1, paragraph 1.)

Before conditioning, the neutral stimulus (light) is called *by Pavlov* an "_____ _____."

"indifferent agent"

---

4

(Refer to Panel R-9-1, paragraph 1.)

DRAW the paradigm for the conditioning described in paragraph 1. (Do not use symbols; write out the actual stimuli and response.)

food in mouth ⟶ salivation
light ⟋

---

95

## 96 / Reflexes and Conditioned Reflexes

5

(Refer to Panel R-9-1, paragraph 1.)

The light was on for how long? _____
Although it is not specifically stated, the light was on when the food presentation began. Which of these diagrams illustrates the procedure Pavlov used?

(A) CS / US — Time (in ten-second units)

(B) CS / US — Time (in ten-second units)

(C) CS / US — Time (in ten-second units)

---

one-half minute

A

**6**

REVIEW FRAME
CHECK the appropriate boxes below:

|  | Simultaneous | Delay | Trace |
|---|---|---|---|
| CS onset precedes US onset | ☐ | ☐ | ☐ |
| CS and US overlap | ☐ | ☐ | ☐ |
| CS termination precedes US onset | ☐ | ☐ | ☐ |
| CS termination follows US onset | ☐ | ☐ | ☐ |
| CS onset follows US onset | ☐ | ☐ | ☐ |

|  | Simultaneous | Delay | Trace |
|---|---|---|---|
| CS onset precedes US onset | ☒ | ☒ | ☒ |
| CS and US overlap | ☒ | ☒ | ☐ |
| CS termination precedes US onset | ☐ | ☐ | ☒ |
| CS termination follows US onset | ☒ | ☒ | ☐ |
| CS onset follows US onset | ☐ | ☐ | ☐ |

---

**7**

(Refer to Panel R-9-1, paragraph 1.)

Thus, the conditioned reflex was an example of a (☐ simultaneous  ☐ delayed  ☐ trace) conditioning procedure.

delayed

---

**8**

(Refer to Panel R-9-1, paragraph 2.)

Following initial conditioning, the magnitude of the salivary response to the light was _____ drops.

10

---

**9**

(Refer to Panel R-9-1, paragraph 2.)

A new stimulus, a _____, was then added and was paired with the _____.

tone
light *or* CS

---

98 / Reflexes and Conditioned Reflexes

10

(Refer to Panel R-9-1, paragraph 2.)

Was the combination tone-light paired with food?
☐ yes  ☐ no

no

---

11

(Refer to Panel R-9-1, paragraph 2.)

Therefore, we can assume that before conditioning the tone was initially a (☐ neutral  ☐ conditioned) stimulus.

neutral

---

12

(Refer to Panel R-9-1, paragraph 2.)

When the tone and light were first paired, they produced a response of a magnitude (☐ less than  ☐ the same as  ☐ greater than) the response produced by the light alone.

the same as

---

13

(Refer to Panel R-9-1, paragraph 2.)

After several pairings with the light, what power did the tone acquire? _____

the power to elicit salivation
(or equivalent answer)

---

14

(Refer to Panel R-9-1, paragraph 2.)

The effect of pairing the tone and light was that the tone elicited a response whose magnitude was _____ drops.

1 or 2

---

Higher Order Conditioning / 99

15

(Refer to Panel R-9-1, paragraph 2.)

The magnitude of the response to the tone was (☐ less  ☐ more) than the response to the light alone.

less

---

16

(Refer to Panel R-9-1, paragraph 2.)

It was demonstrated that the tone did become a(n) _____ stimulus, although the magnitude of the response to the tone was (☐ less than ☐ greater than) it was to the light.

conditioned
less than

---

17

(Refer to Panel R-9-1, paragraph 3.)

Pavlov reports not only that the magnitude of the response to the tone is less, but also that "if the experiments are continued for some time _____." (COMPLETE the sentence.)

the tone will lose its action

---

18

(Refer to Panel R-9-1.)

The conditioning procedure that Pavlov describes in paragraphs 2 and 3 is called _____ order conditioning.

second

---

19

(Refer to Panel R-9-1.)

There seems to be, then, an additional phenomenon of conditioned reflexes: a neutral stimulus (a tone) has become a conditioned stimulus in spite of the fact that it has never been paired directly with the _____.

US or unconditioned stimulus or food in the mouth

100 / Reflexes and Conditioned Reflexes

**20**

(Refer to Panel R-9-1.)

The tone acquired the power to elicit a response by being paired with another _____ stimulus (a light).

conditioned

---

**21**

(Refer to Panel R-9-1.)

The tone is referred to as a conditioned stimulus of the _____ order.

second

---

**22**

A paradigm describing this procedure of second order conditioning would be:

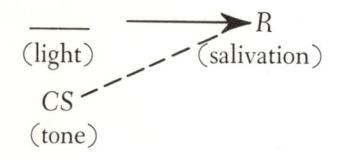

$$\underset{\text{(light)}}{\underline{\quad\quad}} \longrightarrow \underset{\text{(salivation)}}{R}$$
$$\underset{\text{(tone)}}{CS} \nearrow$$

$$\underset{\text{(light)}}{CS} \longrightarrow \underset{\text{(salivation)}}{R}$$
$$\underset{\text{(tone)}}{CS} \nearrow$$

---

**23**

(Refer to Panel R-9-1, paragraph 3.)

The reflex: tone ⟶ salivation is called a reflex of the _____ _____.

second order

---

**24**

A conditioned reflex can be established in two ways:

    1. by pairing a conditioned stimulus with an unconditioned stimulus
    2. _____

by pairing a conditioned stimulus with a previously conditioned stimulus (or equivalent answer)

25

If an initially neutral stimulus is paired with a conditioned stimulus, the neutral stimulus can become a stimulus of the _____ order, and the resultant reflex is called a _____.

second
reflex of the second order

------------------------------

26

One important characteristic of a second order reflex is that the magnitude of the response is considerably (☐ less  ☐ greater) than the magnitude of the response in a first order reflex.

less

------------------------------

27

Magnitude and latency are inversely related. That means that as magnitude decreases, latency _____.

increases

------------------------------

28

If the magnitude of the response to the second order CS is smaller than the magnitude of the response to the first order CS, you might predict that the latency of the response to the second order CS would be (☐ shorter  ☐ longer) than that to the first order CS.

longer

------------------------------

29

Another property of a second order reflex is that if the experiment is continued for some time, the response to the second order CS will _____.

disappear *or* drop out *or* lose its action *or* decrease (or equivalent answer)

------------------------------

102 / Reflexes and Conditioned Reflexes

30

(Refer to Panel R-9-1.)

What happened to the magnitude of the response as the experiment progressed from lower order to higher order conditioning?

The magnitude:
- ☐ increased
- ☐ decreased

decreased

------------------------------------------------

31

The transitory nature of the second order reflex and the small magnitude of the response led Pavlov to raise some doubt as to the actual existence of second order reflexes.

**NO RESPONSE REQUIRED**

**NO RESPONSE REQUIRED; GO ON TO NEXT FRAME.**

------------------------------------------------

32

One or two of Pavlov's pupils have reported third and higher order conditioned reflexes. A third order conditioned reflex would require that an initially neutral stimulus be paired only with a conditioned stimulus of the _____ order.

second

------------------------------------------------

33

Experiments in recent years have not been able to reproduce these experiments on conditioned reflexes above the second order. Considering Pavlov's statements and these recent findings, the existence of higher order reflexes is (☐ likely ☐ unlikely).

unlikely

------------------------------------------------

## 34

Now you should be able to design a complex conditioning experiment.

You are given a dog, a supply of food powder, a buzzer to become the first order CS, and a black cardboard square. You are going to make the square into a second order CS. Your very *first* step toward eventually obtaining a second order conditioned reflex would be to form a conditioned reflex between the _____ and _____.

buzzer (and) food in the mouth

---

## 35

After the buzzer had acquired the eliciting power of a CS, the next step would be to _____.

pair the black square with the buzzer

---

## 36

To demonstrate clearly and unquestionably that you had produced *second order* conditioning, you must be careful never to pair the _____ _____ with the _____.

black square
food in the mouth (US)

---

## 37

By the way, there is something else you should have done. You should have shown that *before* conditioning, neither the buzzer nor the black square _____ salivation.

elicited

---

## 38

To show that the buzzer and square were originally neutral stimuli, you could, in test trials before conditioning, present the buzzer or black square and observe if _____ occurred.

salivation

## 39

If no salivation occurred, then you could properly state: "The *CS*'s were originally _____ stimuli."

neutral

---

## 40

*To review:* All the conditioning procedures that we have described thus far have one important feature in common: in every case, there is pairing between two _____.

stimuli

---

## 41

To obtain the simple first order conditioned reflex, it is necessary to pair _____.

a *CS* with a *US*

---

## 42

Two steps are involved in the formation of a second order conditioned reflex. First, a *CS* is paired with a *US* until a conditioned reflex is formed. Second, _____.

a new *CS* is paired with the *CS* until this *CS* acquires eliciting power (or equivalent answer)

---

## 43

By definition, a neutral stimulus will not elicit the response prior to _____.

conditioning

---

## 44

The whole object of the conditioning procedure is to form a _____ reflex. We know that conditioning has taken place when a stimulus which was initially _____ has acquired the eliciting power of, and can be substituted for, the _____.

new *or* conditioned

neutral

*US*

45

We know we have a conditioned reflex when the CS _____ the _____.

elicits (the) response or R

46

The response is measured in terms of its _____ and its _____.

latency } either
magnitude } order

47

REVIEW

CHECK the appropriate box to indicate whether each of the following variables is dependent or independent:

|  | Dependent | Independent | Dependent | Independent |
|---|---|---|---|---|
| Latency | ☐ | ☐ | ☒ | ☐ |
| Magnitude | ☐ | ☐ | ☒ | ☐ |
| Number of pairings | ☐ | ☐ | ☐ | ☒ |
| Order of conditioning | ☐ | ☐ | ☐ | ☒ |
| Intensity | ☐ | ☐ | ☐ | ☒ |

## 106 / Reflexes and Conditioned Reflexes

**48**

Thus far we have dealt with many stimuli and many responses.

There are more stimuli and responses in this and the following frames. You will be asked to INDICATE whether there is a reflex, and, if there is, to COMPLETE the paradigm for it by giving the specific stimulus and response, and indicating if the stimulus is a *US* or a *CS*.

For example:

    A small child gets smoke in his eyes while standing near a bonfire and his eyes water.

Is this a reflex?  ☐ yes  ☐ no

If it is a reflex, COMPLETE the paradigm for it below:

_____→_____
(      )  (      )

yes

US ———→ R
(smoke)  (eyes water)
(or equivalent answer)

---

**49**

    A boy runs away from a dog.

Is this a reflex?  ☐ yes  ☐ no

_____→_____
(      )  (      )

no

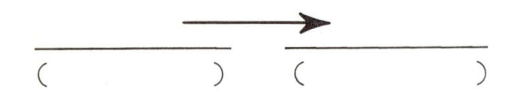

    The sound of the dentist's drill causes a man to perspire.

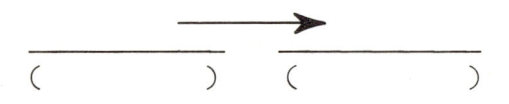

Is this a reflex?  ☐ yes  ☐ no

_____→_____
(      )  (      )

yes

CS ———→ R
(sound of  (perspiring)
drill)
(or equivalent answer)

50

Here is a brief description of an incident:

> As it was growing dark and cold, two boys were playing a game of catch. The cold wind raised "goose bumps" on their arms. Soon, their mother called them for dinner. When they heard her, they began to run to the house and their mouths began to water. As they entered the brightly lit house, their pupils, which had expanded in the dark, contracted in the light. As they were seated at dinner, one of them spilled a glass of milk. When their dessert was brought, the boys grabbed for it, and as a result their mother scolded them.

Now, DIAGRAM the reflexes in the incident described.

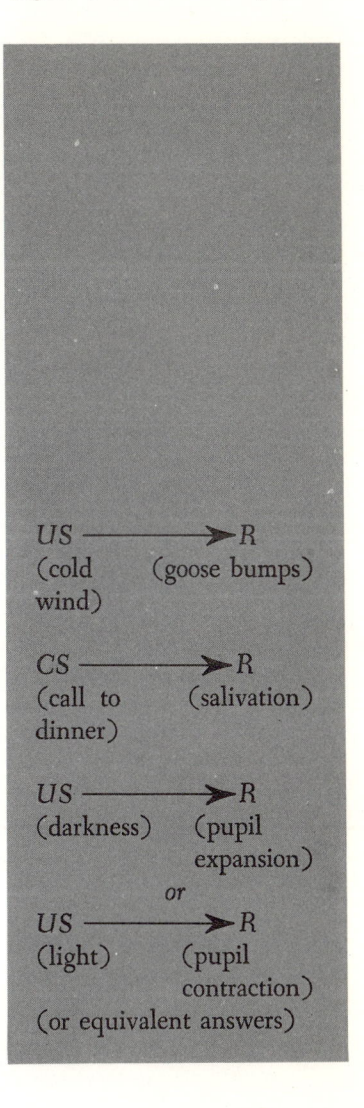

---

US ⟶ R
(cold wind) (goose bumps)

CS ⟶ R
(call to dinner) (salivation)

US ⟶ R
(darkness) (pupil expansion)

*or*

US ⟶ R
(light) (pupil contraction)

(or equivalent answers)

# PANEL R-2-1

## Pupil Contraction as a Function of Light Intensity

The experimenters, by means of an infrared photography method, were able to photograph and measure pupil contraction either in the light or in the dark. Human subjects were first kept in a darkened chamber for about 30 minutes. During the experimental session, each subject's head was held motionless by a chin rest, upright bar, and eyepiece. Successive spots of light of different intensity were flashed in the eye, and photographs of the eye taken. Each level of intensity was used several times and the results were averaged for that intensity value. In the figure below, the diameter of the pupil is plotted on the vertical axis, above the intensity (brightness) at which each observation was made.

(*From:* Wagman, I. H., and Nathanson, L. M., "Influence of White Light upon Pupil Diameter for the Human and for the Rabbit," in *Proc. Soc. Exp. Biol. Med.*, 49, pp. 466-470.)

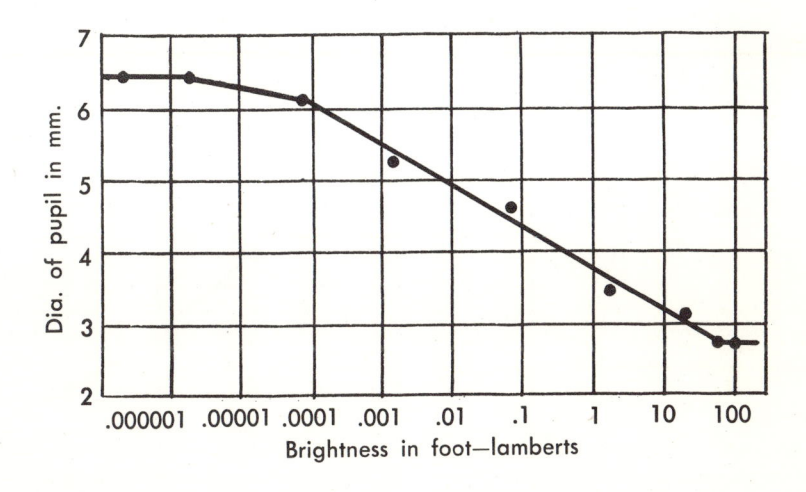

## PANEL R-3-1

A

______________________

______________________

Figure I

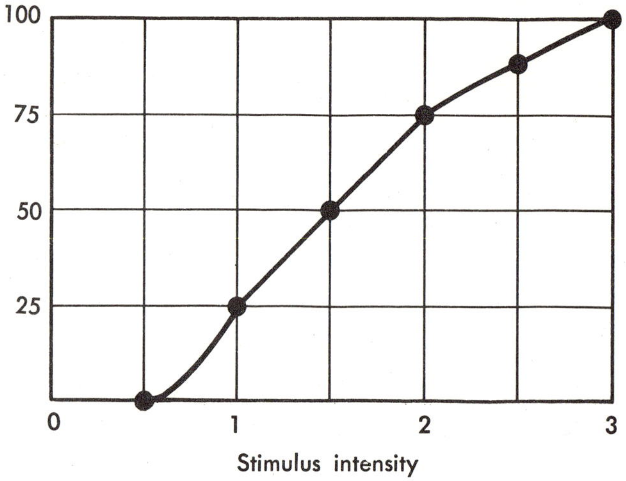

100
75
50
25
0
1
2
3
Stimulus intensity


B

______________________

______________________

Figure II

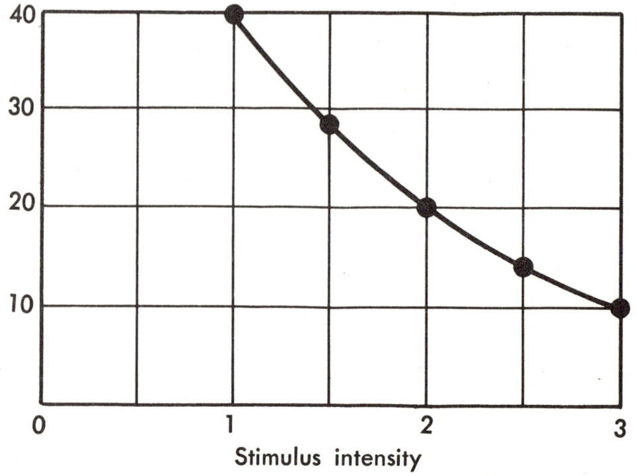

40
30
20
10
0
1
2
3
Stimulus intensity

## PANEL R-7-1

Ivan Pavlov (1849-1936), a Russian physiologist, was the first person to investigate the quantitative properties of conditioned reflexes in the laboratory. The following paragraphs describe one of his experiments with the salivary reflex:

Dogs served as subjects under carefully controlled laboratory conditions. The dog was placed in a harness on a table in a sound-proofed experimental room. Saliva ran from the dog's mouth into a glass measuring tube.

*Session I*

On several occasions food was placed in the dog's mouth. On the average the dog produced 15 drops of saliva each time food was placed in its mouth. Secretion of saliva began two seconds after introduction of the food.

*Session II*

With no food available, a metronome was sounded. No salivation occurred to the metronome.

*Session III*

The metronome was turned on. Five seconds later, food was placed in the dog's mouth. Salivation occurred 2 seconds after the food entered the dog's mouth. The metronome was turned off when the food was in the dog's mouth. This procedure was repeated 10 times. On the fifth trial three drops of saliva were produced 4 seconds after the metronome began. By the tenth repetition the dog began salivating 2 seconds after the metronome began; 10 drops were produced. Thus Pavlov successfully demonstrated conditioning of the salivary reflex.

(Material based on descriptions in: Pavlov, I. P., *Conditioned Reflexes*. New York: Dover Press.)

*Historical Note:* Pavlov's work as a physiologist centered on digestive activity, and for this work he received the Nobel Prize in medicine in 1904. In his laboratory in Petrograd (now Leningrad), he first noticed secretion to "incidental" stimuli, which he then investigated and reported on in *Conditioned Reflexes* and later work.

# PANEL R-7-2

F. S. Keller and W. N. Schoenfeld give the following account of an experiment by G. V. Anrep, one of Pavlov's pupils. The experiment was reported in 1920. Once again, the subject was a dog, and the salivary reflex was studied.

In this study, a tone of 637.5 cycles per second was sounded for a 5-second stimulation period; 2 or 3 seconds later the dog was given biscuit powder. At intervals of 5 to 35 minutes, this pairing was repeated. In 16 days, 50 such combinations were presented and 6 tests were made with the tone alone. The test tone was of 30 seconds' duration, and Anrep measured response magnitude by the number of drops of saliva that were secreted in this period. In addition, he recorded the latencies of the response, in seconds.

The results of the experiment are recorded in the table.

### ACQUISITION OF A CONDITIONED SALIVARY REFLEX

| Number of Paired Stimulations | Response Magnitude (drops of saliva) | Response Latency (seconds) |
|---|---|---|
| 1 | 0 | — |
| 10 | 6 | 18 |
| 20 | 20 | 9 |
| 30 | 60 | 2 |
| 40 | 62 | 1 |
| 50 | 59 | 2 |

(From: Keller, F. S., and Schoenfeld, W. N., *Principles of Psychology*. New York: Appleton-Century-Crofts, 1950, p. 18.)

# PANEL R-9-1

The following is another description of an experiment done by Pavlov in his laboratory:

1. A light is made a conditioned stimulus for salivation. This is accomplished in the following manner. The dog is put into a dark room, and at a certain moment a bright light is switched on. We wait for half a minute, and then give the dog food and allow it to eat for half a minute. This procedure is repeated several times. Finally the electric light, which at first was an indifferent agent for the animal, and had no relation whatever to the function of the salivary gland, owing to repeated coincidence of eating with salivary activity, becomes endowed with the property of acting as a special stimulus for the salivary gland. Every time the electric light appears we have a salivary secretion. Now we can say that the light has become a conditioned stimulus of the gland. The activity of the salivary gland in such a case serves as a simple reflex of the animal to the external world. This reflex gradually grows until it finally attains a certain limit, in the present case, ten drops of saliva in half a minute.

2. Now we add to the light a definite tone (of about 426 cycles per second). The combination of light and tone lasts a half minute. This combination of stimuli is never accompanied by feeding. For the first few applications of this combination there is no change in the original effect of the light, i.e., the light plus tone gives the same salivary secretion as the light alone did (ten drops in half a minute). I wish to emphasize that this combination is never accompanied by food. And after four or five applications of this combination (without feeding), the tone had acquired the property of acting as a stimulus of the salivary secretion. It is true the effect was very small, only one or two drops.

3. It is evident that the tone acquired its exciting effect by being applied simultaneously with the light, and it has actually gone through the same process as occurred when the light received (from its association with eating) its stimulatory effect on the salivary secretion. In the action of the tone we see the action of a new conditioned reflex, and as in the given case the effect of the tone came about owing to its coincidence with a conditioned stimulus (light) and not to coincidence with an unconditioned stimulus (food), this new stimulator (tone) can be designated as a stimulus of the second order, and the new reflex as a *reflex of the second order*. This effect, it is necessary to note, is in most cases very weak, only one or two drops, very transitory, and not fixed. If the experiments are continued for some time, the tone will lose its action. The secretory action itself is so small and it requires such exact conditions for its manifestation, that doubt may arise even as to its very existence.

(Adapted from: Pavlov, I. P., *Lectures on Conditioned Reflexes.* New York: International Publishers, 1928, pp. 104-105.)

# PSYCHOLOGY I

# TERMINAL EXAMINATION

1. **Reflex Conditioning**

    1. What two things are necessary to make up a reflex?

        a. _____

        b. _____

    2. DEFINE terms *a.* and *b.* and DESCRIBE how they are related in a reflex.

        a. _____

        b. _____

    3. If stimulus intensity is increased, response magnitude
        - ☐ increases
        - ☐ decreases

        If stimulus intensity is increased, response latency
        - ☐ increases
        - ☐ decreases

        CHOOSE the correct relationship:

        |  | Response magnitude | Response latency |
        |---|---|---|
        | stimulus intensity | ☐ direct ☐ inverse | ☐ direct ☐ inverse |
        | number of pairings | ☐ direct ☐ inverse | ☐ direct ☐ inverse |

    4. DEFINE:

        *Threshold* _____

        *Subliminal stimulus* _____

        *Supraliminal stimulus* _____

    5. If a stimulus is weak the response it elicits would have a (☐ long ☐ short) latency and a (☐ strong ☐ weak) magnitude.

6. DRAW and LABEL the paradigm for an unconditioned reflex.

   To what technical term does the arrow refer? _____

7. The title of a psychological study often states the dependent and independent variables. In each of the titles below UNDERLINE the dependent variable with one line and the independent variable with two lines.
   a. A study of the effect on muscular coordination in typewriting as a function of various amounts of alcohol drunk previously.
   b. The effect of various drugs upon patterns of web-weaving by a spider.
   c. Does lack of light in infancy affect visual ability in later life?
   d. Is fear (cringing, crying, etc.) in a young chimpanzee reduced when the chimpanzee's mother is present in the cage?
   e. What are the color patterns necessary to set off aggression in the Siamese fighting fish?
   f. The effects of continued test trials on a second order reflex.
   g. Changes in the latency of a conditioned reflex as a function of number of pairings between the CS and the US.

8. What is the major difference between an unconditioned and a conditioned stimulus? _____

9. Briefly describe the procedure you would use to make a reflex in which a handshake produced salivation. (Use a diagram if you find it helpful.) _____

10. *a.* What is the name of the procedure of pairing an unconditioned and a neutral stimulus? _____

   *b.* What is the result of this procedure? _____


11. In a reflex conditioning experiment, how would you demonstrate that the conditioned stimulus was originally neutral? _____


12. As conditioning progresses

   *a.* The latency of the response to the CS
   - ☐ increases
   - ☐ decreases

   *b.* The magnitude of the response to the CS
   - ☐ increases
   - ☐ decreases

13. *a.* DESCRIBE the procedure of higher order conditioning by the use of an example. _____

   *b.* WRITE the paradigms involved using the stimuli and response from your example. _____


14. What are the three types of Pavlovian conditioning procedures which depend on the CS ⟶ US interval?

   *a.* _____
   *b.* _____
   *c.* _____

   Briefly describe the differences between these procedures.
   _____